I0017705

i

This guide is dedicated to unraveling the full potential of Microsoft Word, offering a thorough, step-by-step journey through its rich features and functionalities. From foundational skills to advanced techniques, this book is designed to equip you with the confidence and expertise to create polished, professional documents with ease.

Whether you're taking your first steps, expanding your knowledge, or seeking to refine your skills, this resource is meant for you. May it enhance your creativity, improve your efficiency, and guide you toward mastering Microsoft Word with clarity and confidence.

Table of Contents

Chapter 1: Introduction to Microsoft Word

What is Microsoft Word?

Microsoft Word, often referred to as simply "Word," is one of the most widely used word-processing applications in the world. Developed by Microsoft as part of the Office suite, Word enables users to create, edit, format, and share a wide variety of text-based documents. From simple notes and essays to professional reports and dynamic newsletters, Word's capabilities make it an indispensable tool for personal, academic, and professional use.

At its core, Microsoft Word functions as a digital typewriter—but it is so much more than that. With features like spell checking, grammar suggestions, and formatting tools, it simplifies the writing process. Advanced functionalities such as collaboration tools, template options, and mail merge capabilities elevate its utility, allowing users to create polished and effective documents for any purpose.

Why Microsoft Word is Essential

In an increasingly digital age, the ability to use Microsoft Word is a foundational skill. Whether you're drafting a resume, preparing a business proposal, or creating a personal journal, Word's versatility makes it the go-to tool for document creation. Here are several reasons why Microsoft Word remains essential:

1. **Universal Compatibility**: Word documents are recognized and supported by countless devices, software applications, and platforms. This universal compatibility ensures your work can be accessed and shared effortlessly.
2. **Professional Standard**: In workplaces and educational institutions, Word is often the default software for creating reports, letters, and presentations. Knowing how to use it proficiently is often a requirement in many job roles.
3. **Efficiency**: Features like predefined templates, keyboard shortcuts, and smart suggestions save users time, making it easier to produce high-quality documents in a fraction of the time.
4. **Collaboration Capabilities**: With tools like real-time editing, comments, and tracking changes, Word facilitates seamless collaboration among teams, whether they're in the same office or scattered across the globe.
5. **Customizability**: Word is designed to cater to various user needs. Whether you're a student preparing a thesis, a small business owner designing flyers, or a novelist drafting a manuscript, Word's wide range of tools ensures it can adapt to your specific requirements.
6. **Integration**: Word integrates effortlessly with other Microsoft Office tools, such as Excel and PowerPoint, as well

as cloud services like OneDrive, enabling users to work across platforms and applications without disruption.

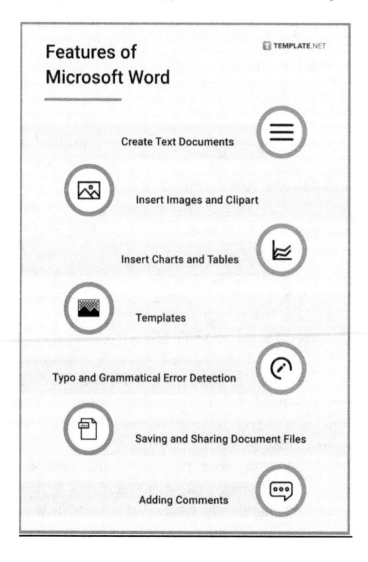

<u>Overview of the Book's Approach</u>

This book is designed to guide you through every aspect of Microsoft Word, from the basics to advanced features. Whether you're a complete beginner or someone looking to sharpen your skills, you'll find detailed instructions and practical examples to help you achieve mastery.

Here's how the book is structured:

1. **Foundational Knowledge**: The first few chapters focus on the basics, including navigating the interface, saving documents, and performing fundamental tasks like typing and editing text.
2. **Intermediate Skills**: Once the basics are covered, we'll dive into topics such as formatting, layout design, and working with tables, charts, and visual elements.
3. **Advanced Features**: You'll learn about collaboration tools, macros, mail merge, and other advanced functionalities that can make your workflow more efficient and professional.
4. **Practical Application**: Throughout the book, we'll include exercises and projects to reinforce learning, such as creating resumes, newsletters, and reports.
5. **Troubleshooting and Tips**: We'll also address common challenges and share time-saving shortcuts, ensuring you're equipped to handle any issues that arise while using Word.

What to Expect from This Book

- **Detailed Instructions**: Each feature is explained step by step, with screenshots and illustrations to help you follow along.
- **Real-World Examples**: We've included practical scenarios to show you how Microsoft Word can be applied to everyday tasks.
- **Interactive Exercises**: You'll have the opportunity to practice what you've learned with guided exercises at the end of each chapter.
- **Comprehensive Coverage**: From creating your first document to mastering advanced tools, this book covers everything you need to know about Microsoft Word.
- **User-Friendly Approach**: The content is written in plain language, avoiding technical jargon to make learning easy and accessible for everyone.

Who Is This Book For?

This book is tailored for a diverse audience:

- **Beginners**: If you're new to Microsoft Word, this book will provide a comprehensive introduction, ensuring you feel confident from the start.
- **Intermediate Users**: If you already have some experience with Word, this book will help you unlock advanced features and streamline your workflow.

- **Professionals and Students**: Whether you're preparing business documents or academic assignments, this book offers tools and tips to elevate the quality of your work.

By the end of this book, you'll have a thorough understanding of Microsoft Word's capabilities and feel empowered to create professional, polished documents with ease. Let's get started!

Chapter 2: Setting Up Microsoft Word

Microsoft Word is a versatile tool used worldwide for document creation, editing, and formatting. To fully unlock its potential, it's essential to set up Word properly on your device. Whether you're using the desktop application, web version, or mobile app, this chapter will guide you through the installation process, help you understand the different versions of Word, and ensure your system meets the necessary requirements.

Installing Microsoft Word on Your Computer

The first step in using Microsoft Word is installing it on your device. Here's how to do it:

For Windows and macOS Users:

1. **Purchase or Subscribe:**
   - Microsoft Word is available as a standalone product or as part of the Microsoft 365 subscription. Visit the official Microsoft website to choose a plan that suits your needs.
   - If you're part of an organization or educational institution, you may have access to Word at no additional cost through a group license.

2. **Download the Installer:**
   - Log in to your Microsoft account.
   - Go to the Microsoft 365 portal or the Word product page.
   - Click on the **Install** button to download the setup file.
3. **Run the Installer:**
   - Locate the downloaded file (usually in the **Downloads** folder).
   - Double-click the file to launch the installer.
4. **Follow the Installation Wizard:**
   - Choose the installation options, such as default language and directory.
   - Click **Install** and wait for the process to complete.
5. **Activate Word:**
   - Open Word and sign in with your Microsoft account to activate the product.
   - Enter the product key if prompted.

For Mobile Devices (iOS and Android):

Microsoft Word is also available as a mobile app, perfect for on-the-go editing. To install:

1. **Visit the App Store or Google Play Store:**
   - Search for "Microsoft Word."
   - Tap **Download** or **Install**.
2. **Sign In:**
   - Open the app and log in using your Microsoft account.
   - If you have a Microsoft 365 subscription, you'll unlock additional premium features.
3. **Sync with Cloud Storage:**

- Enable integration with OneDrive or other supported cloud storage options for seamless access to your files.

For Web Users:

The web-based version of Word is accessible through a browser. It's a lightweight option that doesn't require installation. To access:

1. Visit Microsoft Office Online.
2. Log in with your Microsoft account.
3. Click on the **Word** icon to start using the web version.

Understanding Word Versions: Desktop, Web, and Mobile

Microsoft Word comes in three primary versions, each tailored for different needs:

Desktop Version:

- **Best For:** Heavy users, professionals, and anyone requiring full access to Word's advanced features.
- **Key Features:**
    - Comprehensive formatting and editing tools.
    - Offline accessibility.
    - Support for add-ins and customizations.
- **Limitations:** Requires installation and a compatible device.

Web Version:

- **Best For:** Casual users, quick edits, and collaboration.
- **Key Features:**
    - Accessible through a browser.
    - Real-time collaboration with multiple users.
    - Auto-saving to OneDrive.
- **Limitations:** Lacks some advanced features available in the desktop version.

Mobile Version:

- **Best For:** On-the-go users and those who need lightweight document editing.
- **Key Features:**
    - Optimized for touchscreen devices.
    - Integration with OneDrive for cloud storage.
    - Basic editing and formatting tools.
- **Limitations:** Some advanced features are not available.

Feature	Desktop	Web	Mobile
Full Features	✔	✖	✖
Cloud Integration	✔	✔	✔
Offline Access	✔	✖	✔

System Requirements and Updates

Ensuring your system meets the necessary requirements is vital for a smooth experience. Here's what you need to know:

System Requirements for the Desktop Version:

1. **Windows:**
   - Operating System: Windows 10 or later.
   - Processor: 1.6 GHz or faster.
   - Memory: 4 GB RAM (64-bit) or 2 GB RAM (32-bit).
   - Hard Disk: At least 4 GB of available space.
   - Display: 1280 x 768 resolution or higher.
2. **macOS:**
   - Operating System: macOS Mojave or later.
   - Processor: Intel or Apple silicon-based Mac.
   - Memory: 4 GB RAM.
   - Hard Disk: At least 10 GB of available space.
   - Display: 1280 x 800 resolution or higher.

System Requirements for Mobile Devices:

- iOS: iOS 14 or later for iPhones and iPads.
- Android: Android 6.0 or later, with at least 1 GB of RAM.

Keeping Word Updated

Microsoft regularly releases updates to improve performance, fix bugs, and introduce new features. Keeping your Word version updated ensures you have access to the latest tools and security enhancements. Here's how to update:

1. **Desktop:**
   - Open any Office app, such as Word.
   - Click **File** > **Account** > **Update Options** > **Update Now.**

2. **Mobile:**
   - o Go to your device's app store and check for updates under the **Updates** section.
3. **Web:**
   - o The web version is always up-to-date, so no action is needed.

Tips for a Smooth Setup Experience

1. **Backup Important Files:**
   - o Before installing or updating Word, ensure your documents are backed up, especially if you're transitioning to a new device.
2. **Enable Cloud Sync:**
   - o Linking Word to OneDrive ensures your documents are automatically saved and accessible from any device.
3. **Familiarize Yourself with Licensing:**
   - o Understand whether your version of Word is a one-time purchase or part of a subscription. This affects your access to updates and additional features.

Chapter 3: Exploring the Microsoft Word Interface

Microsoft Word's interface is designed to be intuitive and user-friendly, allowing you to create documents with ease. However, to fully unlock its potential, it's important to familiarize yourself with its various components. In this chapter, we'll take a detailed tour of Word's interface, highlighting its features and how to customize it for your specific needs.

Opening Microsoft Word for the First Time

When you launch Microsoft Word for the first time, you're greeted with the **Start Screen**, which provides a central hub for accessing documents and templates. Here's what you'll find:

1. **Recent Documents**: A list of files you've worked on recently, allowing you to quickly reopen them.
2. **Templates**: Pre-designed templates for various types of documents such as resumes, letters, and reports.
3. **Search Bar**: A convenient way to search for additional templates or features online.
4. **Blank Document**: The option to start with a completely blank slate, which is the most common choice for new projects.

To start working, click on **Blank Document** or select a template that suits your needs. Once you've entered the main workspace, it's time to explore Word's interface.

Overview of the Ribbon and Tabs

The **Ribbon** is the primary toolbar in Microsoft Word, housing all the tools and features you'll use. It's located at the top of the window and is divided into **Tabs**, each grouping related commands. Let's explore the most commonly used tabs:

1. **Home Tab**:
   - Contains basic text editing tools like font styles, sizes, bold, italic, underline, alignment, and line spacing.
   - Includes options for clipboard actions such as **Cut**, **Copy**, and **Paste**.
2. **Insert Tab**:
   - Used for adding elements to your document, such as pictures, tables, shapes, hyperlinks, and headers or footers.
   - Includes advanced features like adding charts, SmartArt, and WordArt.
3. **Design Tab**:
   - Provides tools for changing the overall appearance of your document, such as themes, colors, and fonts.
   - Useful for creating visually appealing layouts.
4. **Layout Tab**:
   - Focused on page-level adjustments like margins, orientation, size, columns, and spacing.
5. **References Tab**:

- o Ideal for academic or professional documents, offering tools to insert citations, bibliographies, tables of contents, and footnotes.
6. **Review Tab**:
   - o Enables collaborative features like adding comments, tracking changes, and performing spell and grammar checks.
7. **View Tab**:
   - o Controls how your document is displayed on the screen, offering options like Read Mode, Print Layout, and Web Layout.
   - o Includes tools like rulers, gridlines, and navigation panes.

Each tab is further divided into **Groups**, organizing related commands. For example, the **Font** group in the Home tab contains font-related options like size, style, and color.

The Quick Access Toolbar

The **Quick Access Toolbar** is a small customizable toolbar located above or below the Ribbon. It provides one-click access to frequently used commands. By default, it includes options like **Save**, **Undo**, and **Redo**.

To customize the Quick Access Toolbar:

1. Click the small drop-down arrow at the right end of the toolbar.
2. Select the commands you want to add from the menu, such as **Print**, **New**, or **Open**.

3. For additional options, click **More Commands**, which opens a dialog box where you can select from a comprehensive list of features.

The Status Bar and Zoom Controls

The **Status Bar** is located at the bottom of the Word window and provides useful information about your document, such as:

- **Page Count**: Displays the current page number and the total number of pages.
- **Word Count**: Shows the total number of words in your document.
- **Language**: Indicates the language being used for spell and grammar checks.
- **View Modes**: Allows you to switch between different views, such as Print Layout and Web Layout.

Next to the Status Bar, you'll find the **Zoom Controls**. These let you adjust the zoom level of your document for better visibility:

- **Zoom Slider**: Drag the slider left or right to zoom out or in.
- **Percentage Box**: Click the percentage box to manually enter a zoom level.

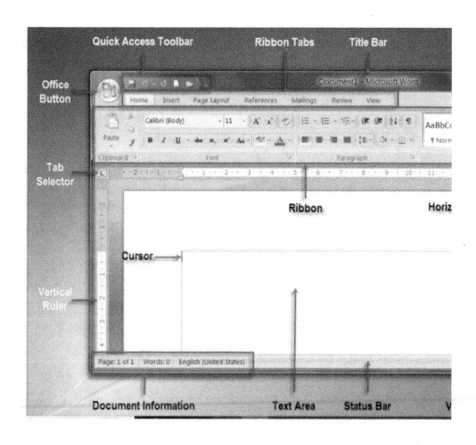

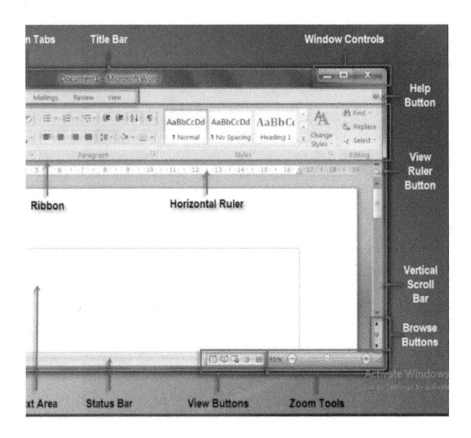

Customizing the Interface for Your Needs

Microsoft Word's interface can be tailored to suit your workflow, making it more efficient and user-friendly. Here's how to customize key elements:

1. **Ribbon Customization**:
   o Right-click anywhere on the Ribbon and select **Customize the Ribbon**.
   o Add or remove tabs and groups, or create your own custom tabs to group frequently used commands.

2. **Changing Themes**:
   o Click **File > Options > General**.
   o Under the **Office Theme** section, choose from options like **Colorful**, **Dark Gray**, or **White** to match your preferences.
3. **Adjusting the Status Bar**:
   o Right-click on the Status Bar to bring up a list of options.
   o Check or uncheck items to control what information is displayed.
4. **Keyboard Shortcuts**:
   o If you rely heavily on specific commands, consider learning or customizing keyboard shortcuts. Go to **File > Options > Customize Ribbon > Keyboard Shortcuts**.

Chapter 4: Starting a New Document

Creating a new document is the very first step in using Microsoft Word. Whether you're starting from scratch, using a pre-designed template, or working on multiple files at once, Word makes it easy to organize your work and hit the ground running. This chapter will take you through each process, offering detailed insights to help you confidently navigate this crucial stage.

Opening a Blank Document

The most basic and common way to start a new project in Word is by opening a blank document. This option provides a clean slate for any type of document you wish to create.

Steps to Open a Blank Document:

1. **Launch Microsoft Word**: Open the Word application on your device. If it's your first time opening Word, you'll be taken directly to the start screen.
2. **Choose "Blank Document"**: On the start screen, you'll see various options for starting a new project. Click on the large white rectangle labeled **"Blank Document"**. This opens a fresh, unformatted page ready for your input.
3. **Set Up Your Workspace**: Before typing, you might want to adjust basic settings like margins, font style, and page layout

to suit your needs. These settings can be modified later as well.

Tips for Blank Documents:

- Use blank documents for projects where you want full creative control over formatting and layout.
- If you often use the same settings, consider creating and saving a custom template for faster setup next time.

Using Templates for Quick Setups

Microsoft Word's templates are a game-changer for users who want a professional look without spending time on complex formatting. Templates are pre-designed documents tailored for specific purposes, such as resumes, reports, newsletters, or invitations.

Benefits of Using Templates:

- Save time by eliminating the need to set up formatting manually.
- Ensure a polished and consistent appearance.
- Access to industry-standard designs that can elevate your document's quality.

How to Use Templates in Word:

1. **Access Templates**: When you open Word, go to the start screen and click on **"More templates"**. Alternatively, navigate to **File > New** from the top menu bar.

2. **Browse or Search Templates**: Scroll through the featured templates or use the search bar to find one that fits your needs. For instance, type "invoice" or "flyer" to filter the results.

3. **Select and Open**: Once you find the right template, click on it, and Word will create a new document based on that design.

4. **Customize the Template**: Edit text, replace placeholder images, and tweak colors to personalize the template.

Tips for Effective Template Use:

- Don't hesitate to modify templates to make them uniquely yours.
- Save the edited template for future use if it's something you'll need repeatedly.

Switching Between Documents

Working on multiple documents at the same time is common, especially when cross-referencing information or comparing versions. Microsoft Word makes it simple to manage multiple files simultaneously.

Methods for Switching Documents:

1. **Using the Taskbar**: If you've opened multiple documents, their windows will appear in your taskbar (at the bottom of your screen). Click on the document you want to bring to the forefront.
2. **Using Word's Built-in Switcher**: Go to the **View** tab on the Ribbon and select **Switch Windows**. A dropdown will list all open documents. Click on the desired file to bring it into focus.
3. **Alt+Tab (Windows) or Command+Tab (Mac)**: This keyboard shortcut cycles through all open programs and documents on your computer, making it faster to switch between files.

Tips for Efficient Multi-Document Management:

- Use descriptive file names to avoid confusion when multiple documents are open.
- Arrange the windows side by side for easier comparison. Go to the **View** tab and click **View Side by Side** to enable this feature.
- Save each document frequently to prevent data loss, especially when working on multiple files.

Best Practices for Starting a Document

Here are some additional tips to help you start new documents efficiently and effectively:

- **Plan Before You Begin**: If you know the structure of your document in advance, it will save time later. For instance, decide on the page layout, fonts, and styles before typing.
- **Name Your Document Early**: Instead of leaving your file as "Document1," save it with a meaningful name immediately. This helps you locate it easily later.
- **Leverage Cloud Storage**: Save your document on OneDrive or another cloud service to access it from any device and ensure you don't lose your work.

Practical Example

Let's say you're tasked with writing a business report. Here's how you could approach starting the document:

1. **Step 1: Choose a Template**
   Search for "business report" in Word's template gallery to find a suitable design.
2. **Step 2: Customize the Template**
   Replace placeholder text with your content. Adjust colors to match your company branding.
3. **Step 3: Save Your Work**
   Save the file as "Q1 Business Report 2025.docx" to keep it organized.

4. **Step 4: Switch Between Related Documents**
   Open previous reports for reference and use the **Switch Windows** feature to toggle between them effortlessly.

Chapter 5: Saving and Opening Documents

I n Microsoft Word, saving and accessing your work is fundamental to maintaining an organized workflow and ensuring you don't lose important documents. This chapter will explore the essentials of saving and opening files, covering different saving options, file formats, AutoSave, recovery options, and tips for file organization.

Understanding Save vs. Save As: Key Differences

At first glance, the commands **Save** and **Save As** might seem interchangeable, but each serves a distinct purpose:

1. **Save**:
   - This option is used to update the current version of your document with any changes you've made.
   - Think of it as overwriting the file in its existing location.
   - Shortcut: **Ctrl+S** (Windows) or **Command+S** (Mac).

   Example: If you're editing a report called *Monthly Budget.docx*, pressing **Save** will replace the original file with the latest updates.

2. **Save As**:

- This option allows you to create a new version of your document while preserving the original file.
- It's ideal for saving under a new name, in a different location, or in another file format.
- Shortcut: **F12** (Windows) or **Command+Shift+S** (Mac).

Example: You could use **Save As** to save *Monthly Budget.docx* as *Monthly Budget - Final.pdf.*

Alternatively, you can click the **File** tab, and select **Save** or **Save As**

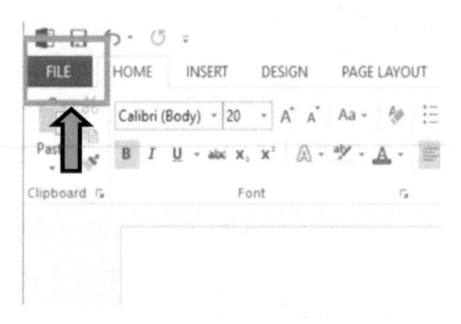

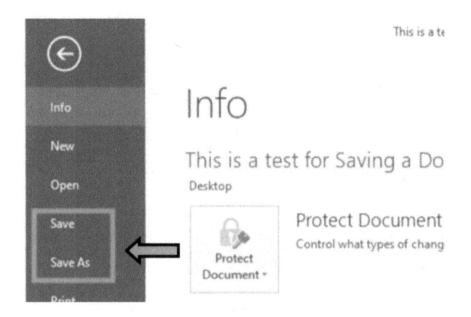

Exploring File Formats

Microsoft Word supports various file formats to cater to different needs. Here's an overview of the most commonly used ones:

1. **DOCX**:
   - The default Word format, offering full compatibility with Word's features.
   - Ideal for editing and sharing documents with collaborators who use Word.
2. **PDF (Portable Document Format)**:
   - Preserves the layout and formatting of your document, ensuring it appears the same on any device.
   - Perfect for distributing read-only files or professional documents like resumes.

- To save as a PDF, select **File > Save As > Choose PDF from the dropdown menu**.

3. **TXT (Plain Text)**:
   - Saves your document without formatting, leaving only the raw text.
   - Useful for importing text into coding environments or basic applications.

4. **RTF (Rich Text Format)**:
   - A format that retains basic formatting (like bold and italic) but is more universally compatible than DOCX.

5. **Other Formats**:
   - **HTML**: Saves the document as a webpage.
   - **ODT**: Compatible with OpenOffice or LibreOffice.
   - **Template Formats**: Saves your document as a reusable template.

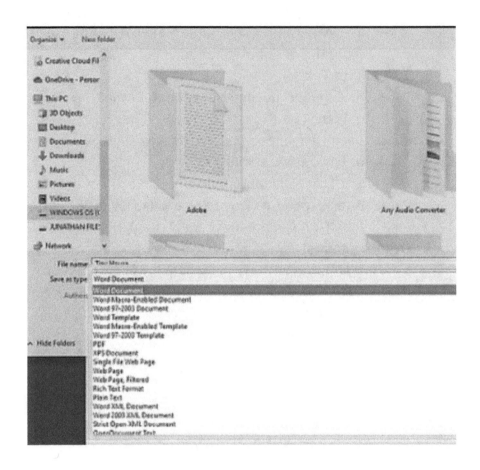

AutoSave: A Lifesaver for Your Work

AutoSave is a feature in Microsoft Word that automatically saves your document at regular intervals. It's particularly useful for protecting your work in case of unexpected shutdowns or errors.

1. **Enabling AutoSave:**

- o If your document is saved in a cloud location like OneDrive or SharePoint, AutoSave is enabled by default.
- o Toggle AutoSave on or off via the switch in the top-left corner of the window.

2. **Recovering Unsaved Work**:
   - o If Word crashes or your computer shuts down, you can recover your unsaved documents.
   - o Steps to recover:
     - Open Word and go to **File > Info > Manage Document > Recover Unsaved Documents**.
     - Select the desired file from the list and click **Open**.

3. **Adjusting AutoSave Intervals**:
   - o To customize how often Word saves your work:
     - Go to **File > Options > Save**.
     - Adjust the **Save AutoRecover information every X minutes** setting.

Organizing Files with Folders

Keeping your documents organized is crucial for productivity, especially when managing multiple projects or versions of the same file.

1. **Creating Folders**:
   - o Organize your files by creating folders based on categories like projects, clients, or dates.
   - o To create a new folder while saving a file:
     - Click **Save As > Browse > New Folder**.

2. **Naming Conventions**:
   o Use descriptive file names to make your documents easier to locate.
   o Examples:
      ▪ *MeetingNotes_2025_01_03.docx.*
      ▪ *ClientProposal_V2.pdf.*
3. **Using Cloud Storage**:
   o Cloud services like OneDrive or SharePoint offer easy access to your files from any device.
   o They also provide built-in version history, allowing you to view or restore previous iterations of your documents.
4. **File Organization Tips**:
   o **Sort by Date**: When working on time-sensitive projects, sorting files by their last modified date can help.
   o **Tagging**: Add tags or keywords to your documents' properties to make them searchable.
   o **Archive Old Files**: Move older, less frequently used documents to an archive folder to declutter your workspace.

Practical Example: Saving and Organizing a Project

Imagine you're drafting a report for a client:

1. **Step 1**: Create a new folder called *Client Reports* in your preferred storage location.
2. **Step 2**: Within that folder, create subfolders like *Drafts, Final Versions*, and *Resources*.

3. **Step 3**: Save the initial version of your report as *ClientReport_Draft1.docx* in the *Drafts* folder.
4. **Step 4**: Use **Save As** to create a polished version named *ClientReport_Final.docx*, saved in the *Final Versions* folder.
5. **Step 5**: Export the final document as a PDF for sharing, ensuring the layout remains intact across devices.

Chapter 6: Navigating a Document

Effectively navigating through a document is an essential skill when working with Microsoft Word. Whether you're handling a short memo or a lengthy manuscript, the ability to quickly locate, review, and modify sections of your document can save you valuable time and effort. In this chapter, we'll explore the tools Word provides to help you move through your document seamlessly, locate specific content, and make precise changes.

Using Scrollbars and Navigation Panes

Navigating through your document is simple when you know how to use the available tools. Two key elements for basic navigation are the **scrollbars** and the **navigation pane**.

1. Using Scrollbars

Scrollbars are located on the right and bottom edges of your document window. They allow you to move through the content with ease, especially in longer documents. Here's how to use them:

- **Vertical Scrollbar**: Found on the right-hand side of the window, this scrollbar lets you move up and down through the document. Click and drag the scrollbar handle to scroll faster, or use the arrows at the top and bottom for smaller movements.

- **Horizontal Scrollbar**: This appears at the bottom of the window if your document contains wide tables, images, or text that extends beyond the default margins. Drag the horizontal scrollbar to move left or right.

Tips for Efficient Scrolling:

- Use the **mouse wheel** to scroll vertically without touching the scrollbar.
- Hold the **Shift key** while using the mouse wheel to scroll horizontally.

2. Enabling and Using the Navigation Pane

The **Navigation Pane** is a powerful tool for navigating large documents. It provides a structured view of your document's headings, pages, or search results, allowing you to jump to specific sections effortlessly.

How to Enable the Navigation Pane:

1. Go to the **View** tab in the Ribbon.
2. In the **Show** group, check the box next to **Navigation Pane**.

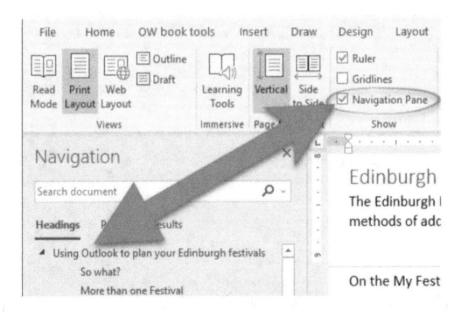

The pane will appear on the left side of your screen with three tabs:

- **Headings**: Displays all headings in the document. Click on any heading to jump to that section.

- **Pages**: Shows thumbnail images of all pages in your document. Clicking a thumbnail takes you to that page.
- **Results**: Displays search results when you use the **Find** feature (explained later).

Why Use the Navigation Pane?

- It's especially useful for documents with multiple sections or chapters.
- It helps you maintain an overview of your document's structure.
- It allows for quick access to specific parts of the document without endless scrolling.

Searching Within a Document Using Find and Replace

The **Find and Replace** tool is indispensable for locating specific words, phrases, or formatting within your document. It's particularly helpful when you need to make global edits or check for consistency.

1. Using the Find Feature

To search for a word or phrase in your document:

1. Press **Ctrl+F** (or **Command+F** on Mac) to open the **Find** pane. Alternatively, click on the **Find** option in the **Editing** group under the **Home** tab.

2. Type the text you're searching for in the search box. As you type, Word will highlight all instances of the text in your document.

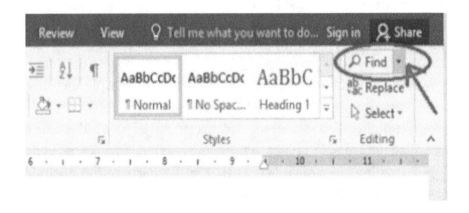

Advanced Search Options:

- Click the **magnifying glass** icon in the Find pane to access advanced options.
- Use checkboxes to match the case (e.g., uppercase vs. lowercase) or find whole words only.

2. Using Replace

The Replace feature allows you to quickly substitute one word or phrase for another throughout the document.

Steps to Use Replace:

1. Press **Ctrl+H** (or **Command+H** on Mac) to open the **Find and Replace** dialog box.

2. In the **Find what** field, type the text you want to locate.
3. In the **Replace with** field, type the replacement text.
4. Click **Replace** to change the first instance or **Replace All** to change all occurrences at once.

Practical Uses:

- Correcting a repeated typo across the document.
- Updating a term or phrase to match current usage.
- Applying consistent formatting to specific words.

Tips:

- Use the **Format** option in the Replace dialog box to replace formatting (e.g., change bold text to italic).
- Click **More >>** in the Replace dialog box to access additional options like searching for special characters (e.g., paragraph marks or tabs).

Using the Go To Feature

The **Go To** feature is ideal for jumping directly to specific locations in your document, such as a particular page, section, or line number.

Accessing Go To:

1. Press **Ctrl+G** (or **Command+G** on Mac) to open the **Go To** tab in the **Find and Replace** dialog box. Alternatively, go to the **Home** tab, click **Find**, and then select **Go To**.

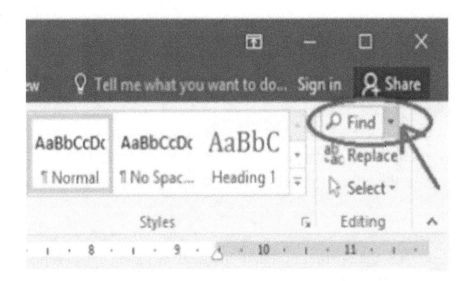

Go To (Ctrl+G)

How to Use Go To:

- In the **Go to what** field, select the type of content you want to navigate to (e.g., Page, Section, Line, Bookmark, Footnote, Comment).
- Enter the specific reference (e.g., page number or bookmark name) in the box.
- Click **Go To** to jump to that location.

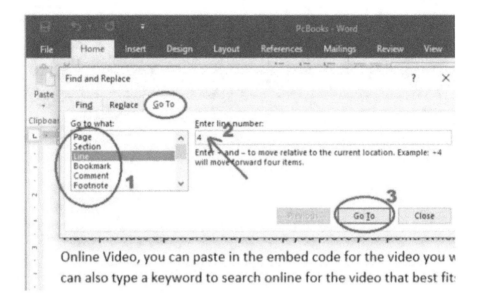

Online Video, you can paste in the embed code for the video you w
can also type a keyword to search online for the video that best fit:

Practical Scenarios:

- Quickly navigate to a specific page in a lengthy report.
- Review all comments or footnotes in one session.
- Jump between bookmarks to review specific sections of a document.

Tips for Efficient Navigation

1. **Combine Navigation Tools**: Use the Navigation Pane for structural overview, Find for specific text, and Go To for precise locations.
2. **Create Bookmarks**: Bookmark important sections of your document for quick access later. To add a bookmark, go to the **Insert** tab, click **Bookmark**, and name the section.
3. **Use Keyboard Shortcuts**: Familiarize yourself with navigation-related shortcuts to work more efficiently.

Mastering these navigation tools will make working with Microsoft Word faster, easier, and more enjoyable. Whether you're scrolling through a short memo or managing a lengthy thesis, these features ensure you can find and edit content without unnecessary frustration. Keep practicing, and soon, navigating even the largest documents will feel second nature!

Chapter 7: Mastering Basic Text Operations

Text operations form the backbone of any work done in Microsoft Word. Whether you're jotting down ideas, crafting an essay, or preparing a professional document, understanding how to work with text efficiently is essential. This chapter will guide you through the foundational tasks of typing, deleting, and manipulating text in Word. With a bit of practice, these skills will become second nature.

Typing Text

Typing in Microsoft Word is straightforward, but mastering its nuances can greatly improve your efficiency:

1. **Cursor Placement**:
   o The blinking vertical bar on your screen is the text cursor. It shows where your next character will appear.
   o You can move the cursor by clicking anywhere in the document or using the **arrow keys** on your keyboard.
2. **Entering Text**:

- Begin typing where the cursor is placed. Microsoft Word automatically wraps text to the next line when you reach the end of the page margins.
- If you need to start a new paragraph, press the **Enter** key.

3. **Line Breaks vs. Paragraph Breaks**:
   - A new paragraph is created by pressing **Enter**, but if you only need to start a new line without a full paragraph break, press **Shift + Enter**.

Deleting Text

Errors are a natural part of writing, but Microsoft Word offers multiple ways to remove unwanted text:

1. **Backspace Key**:
   - Press **Backspace** to delete the character to the left of the cursor.
   - Hold it down to continuously delete multiple characters.
2. **Delete Key**:
   - Press **Delete** to remove the character to the right of the cursor.
3. **Selecting and Deleting**:
   - Highlight a block of text by clicking and dragging your mouse, then press **Delete** or **Backspace** to remove it.
   - This method is faster for deleting large sections of text.

Selecting Text

Selecting text is a key skill that allows you to perform various actions, such as formatting, copying, or deleting. Here's how you can select text in Word:

1. **Mouse Selection**:
   - Click at the start of the text you want to select, hold down the mouse button, and drag to the end of the desired section.
   - Release the button to finalize the selection.
2. **Keyboard Shortcuts**:
   - Hold down the **Shift** key and use the arrow keys to expand or shrink the selection.
   - Press **Ctrl + A** to select the entire document.
3. **Double-Click and Triple-Click**:
   - Double-click on a word to select it.
   - Triple-click within a paragraph to select the entire paragraph.
4. **Advanced Selection**:
   - Hold down the **Ctrl** key while selecting multiple, non-contiguous pieces of text with your mouse. This is particularly useful for formatting specific sections simultaneously.

Cut, Copy, and Paste

Moving or duplicating text is a fundamental aspect of working in Word. These functions save time and effort when reorganizing content.

1. **Cut**:
    - Select the text you want to move.
    - Right-click and choose **Cut**, or use the shortcut **Ctrl + X**.
    - The text will disappear from its original location and be stored in your clipboard, ready to be placed elsewhere.
2. **Copy**:
    - Highlight the desired text.
    - Right-click and select **Copy**, or press **Ctrl + C**.
    - This creates a duplicate in your clipboard without removing the original text.
3. **Paste**:
    - Place your cursor where you want the text to appear.
    - Right-click and select **Paste**, or press **Ctrl + V**.
    - The clipboard's content will be inserted at the cursor's location.
4. **Paste Options**:
    - After pasting, a small clipboard icon appears, offering paste options:
        - **Keep Source Formatting**: Retains the original formatting of the copied text.
        - **Merge Formatting**: Adjusts the text to match the surrounding style.
        - **Keep Text Only**: Removes formatting entirely, leaving plain text.

Undo and Redo: Correcting Mistakes

Mistakes happen, and Microsoft Word provides tools to rectify them instantly:

1. **Undo**:
   - Use the **Undo** feature to reverse your most recent action.
   - Click the **Undo** button in the Quick Access Toolbar or press **Ctrl + Z**.
   - Word keeps a history of your actions, so you can undo multiple steps by repeatedly pressing the shortcut.
2. **Redo**:
   - If you accidentally undo an action, you can restore it using the **Redo** button.
   - Click **Redo** in the Quick Access Toolbar or press **Ctrl + Y**.
3. **Why Undo and Redo Matter**:
   - These tools are invaluable when experimenting with formatting or making significant changes to your document.
   - They allow you to try different options without fear of permanent mistakes.

Tips for Efficient Text Operations

1. **Practice Makes Perfect**:
   - Spend time practicing these functions to build muscle memory, making your workflow smoother and faster.
2. **Keyboard Shortcuts**:

- Learning shortcuts like **Ctrl + X** (Cut), **Ctrl + C** (Copy), and **Ctrl + V** (Paste) can save time and improve productivity.

3. **Clipboard Manager**:
   - Word offers a clipboard feature that stores multiple copied items. You can access it from the **Home** tab by clicking the small arrow in the **Clipboard** group.

Chapter 8: Mastering Text Formatting in Microsoft Word

Formatting text is a fundamental skill that can transform the appearance and readability of your documents. Microsoft Word provides an extensive array of formatting tools, enabling you to emphasize key points, create visually appealing text, and maintain consistency throughout your work. In this chapter, we'll delve deeply into text formatting techniques, ensuring you can make the most of Word's features.

Why Text Formatting Matters

Proper text formatting is not just about aesthetics—it enhances clarity, draws attention to important points, and ensures your document looks professional. Whether you're drafting a formal report, creating an invitation, or designing a flyer, the right formatting can make all the difference.

Changing Fonts, Sizes, and Colors

One of the most noticeable ways to format text is by altering its font style, size, and color. These adjustments help set the tone of your document, whether formal, casual, or creative.

Selecting and Changing Fonts

The font you choose can convey the personality of your document. A formal letter might require a traditional font like **Times New Roman**, while a flyer might benefit from a playful font like **Comic Sans**. To change the font:

1. Highlight the text you want to modify.
2. Go to the **Home** tab.
3. In the **Font** group, click the drop-down arrow next to the current font name.
4. Scroll through the font list or type the name of a specific font.
5. Click your desired font to apply it to the selected text.

Tip: Use fonts sparingly. Stick to one or two complementary fonts to maintain a professional and uncluttered look.

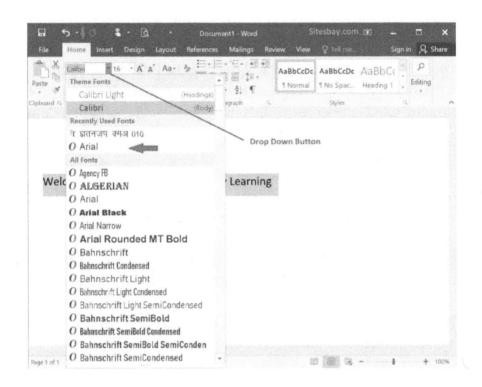

Adjusting Font Sizes

Font size determines how large or small the text appears on the page. Here's how to adjust it:

1. Select the text.
2. In the **Font** group on the **Home** tab, locate the number next to the font name.
3. Click the drop-down arrow and choose a size, or type a specific number for precise control.

Shortcut: Use **Ctrl + Shift + >** to increase the font size and **Ctrl + Shift + <** to decrease it.

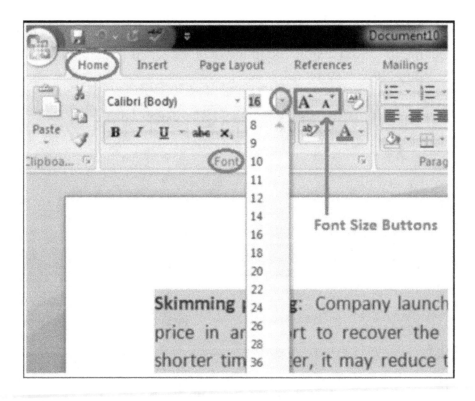

Font Size Buttons

Changing Font Colors

Adding color to text can help it stand out or indicate a specific meaning. For example, red might signal urgency, while green could highlight success.

1. Highlight the text you want to color.
2. Go to the **Font Color** icon in the **Home** tab (it looks like an "A" with a color bar beneath it).
3. Click the drop-down arrow and choose a color from the palette.
4. For additional options, click **More Colors** and select from the advanced color picker.

Tip: Use colors that complement the overall theme of your document. Avoid using too many colors, as this can make the document look chaotic.

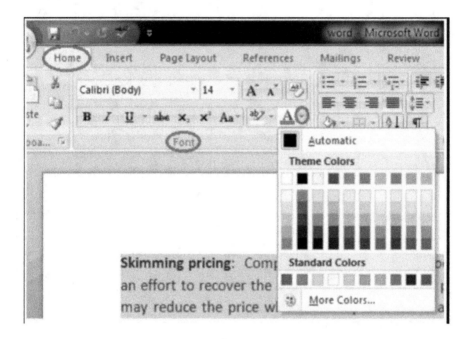

Applying Bold, Italics, Underline, and Other Effects

Emphasizing certain words or phrases can draw the reader's attention to important details. Microsoft Word offers several effects to achieve this.

Using Bold

Bold text is perfect for headings or key points. To make text bold:

- Highlight the text and click the **B** button in the **Font** group.

- Alternatively, press **Ctrl + B** on your keyboard.

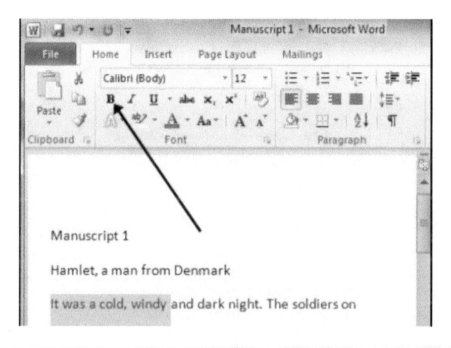

Adding Italics

Italic text can be used for emphasis or to denote titles of works, such as books and movies. To italicize:

- Highlight the text and click the **I** button in the **Font** group.
- Or, press **Ctrl + I**.

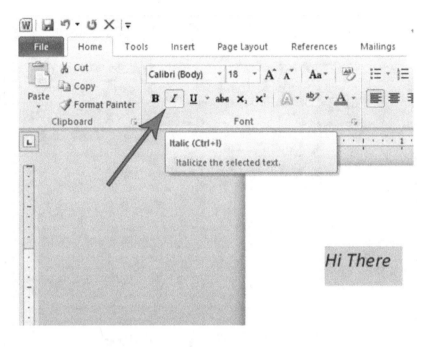

Underlining Text

Underlining is a classic way to emphasize text, often used in printed documents. To underline text:

- Highlight the text and click the **U** button in the **Font** group.
- Or, press **Ctrl + U**.

Tip: To choose a different underline style, click the small arrow next to the **U** button and select from the options.

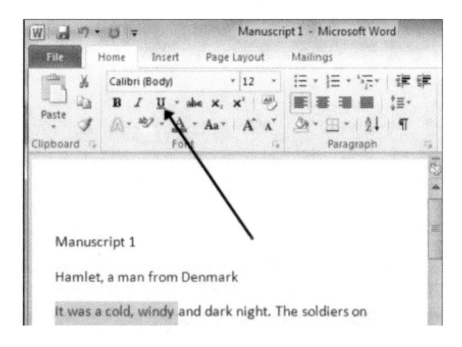

Strikethrough

Use strikethrough to show edits or indicate text that is no longer relevant.

1. Highlight the text.
2. Click the **Strikethrough** button in the **Font** group (visible as "abc" with a line through it).

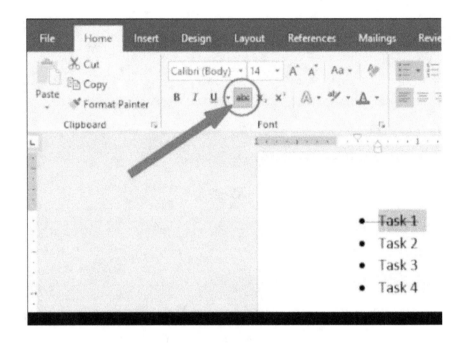

Highlighting Text for Emphasis

Highlighting is a great way to draw attention to specific portions of text, similar to using a marker on paper. To highlight text:

1. Go to the **Home** tab.
2. Locate the **Text Highlight Color** button in the **Font** group.
3. Click the drop-down arrow and select a color.
4. Highlight the desired text.

To remove the highlight, choose **No Color** from the highlight options.

Tip: Use highlighting sparingly to avoid cluttering the document.

Creating Superscripts and Subscripts

Superscripts and subscripts are essential for scientific notation, mathematical equations, and citations.

Using Superscripts

Superscripts are smaller characters positioned above the normal text line. Common uses include exponents (e.g., x^2) or ordinal numbers (e.g., 1st). To apply a superscript:

1. Select the character(s) you want to superscript.
2. Go to the **Home** tab and click the **Superscript** button (x^2 icon) in the **Font** group.
3. Alternatively, press **Ctrl + Shift + +** on your keyboard.

Using Subscripts

Subscripts are smaller characters positioned below the text line, often used in chemical formulas (e.g., H_2O). To apply a subscript:

1. Highlight the character(s) you want to subscript.
2. Click the **Subscript** button (x_2 icon) in the **Font** group under the **Home** tab.
3. Or, press **Ctrl + =** on your keyboard.

<u>Practical Applications of Text Formatting</u>

1. **Professional Documents**: Use a combination of bold and italics for headings and subheadings to create a clean and organized look.
2. **Resumes**: Highlight skills or accomplishments using bold or underline to make them stand out.
3. **Presentations**: Use color and font changes sparingly to emphasize key points while maintaining readability.
4. **Reports**: Incorporate superscripts for citations and subscripts for scientific data.

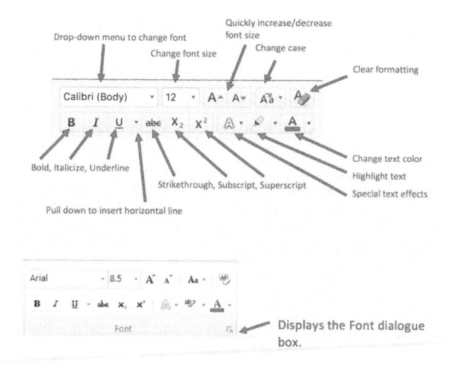

Summary

Text formatting is one of the easiest ways to make your document visually appealing and professional. By mastering these tools, you'll be able to create documents that not only convey your message effectively but also captivate your audience. Practice using different formatting techniques to discover which combinations work best for various types of documents.

Chapter 9: Mastering Paragraph Formatting in Microsoft Word

Formatting paragraphs correctly is one of the key steps to ensure your document looks polished, professional, and easy to read. In this chapter, we'll explore various tools and techniques available in Microsoft Word for paragraph formatting. You'll learn how to adjust alignment, create proper spacing, and enhance your content with lists for better readability.

Paragraph Alignment: Structuring Content Visually

Paragraph alignment determines how text is positioned horizontally across the page. Word offers four alignment options, each serving specific purposes based on your document type.

1. **Left Alignment (Default)**
   - This is the standard alignment in most documents. The text lines up evenly on the left margin, with a ragged edge on the right.
   - **How to apply**: Select the paragraph, then click the **Align Left** button in the **Home** tab or press **Ctrl+L**.
2. **Center Alignment**

- Centered text is often used for titles, headings, or content that needs emphasis. The text is evenly distributed between the left and right margins.
- **How to apply**: Highlight the text and click the **Center** button in the **Home** tab or press **Ctrl+E**.

3. **Right Alignment**
   - Text aligned to the right is commonly used for specific elements like captions, side notes, or signatures.
   - **How to apply**: Select the desired text and click the **Align Right** button in the **Home** tab or press **Ctrl+R**.

4. **Justified Alignment**
   - Justification ensures that text is evenly distributed between the left and right margins, creating a clean, block-like appearance. This is ideal for formal documents such as reports or essays.
   - **How to apply**: Highlight the text and click the **Justify** button in the **Home** tab or press **Ctrl+J**.

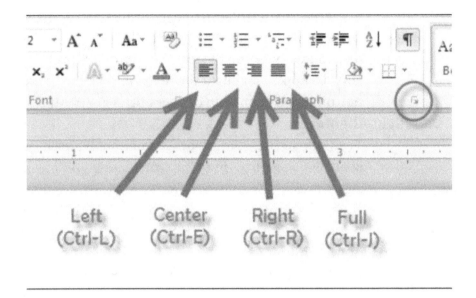

Left (Ctrl-L) Center (Ctrl-E) Right (Ctrl-R) Full (Ctrl-J)

Tip: Overusing justified alignment can sometimes create awkward spacing between words. Use it judiciously for the best visual impact.

Indenting Paragraphs: Enhancing Structure

Indentation helps to visually separate sections of text, making it easier for readers to follow. Word offers several ways to indent paragraphs effectively.

1. **First-Line Indent**
   - This is common in academic and narrative writing, where the first line of a paragraph is pushed inward.
   - **How to apply**:
     a. Select the paragraph.
     b. Open the **Paragraph** dialog box (click the small

arrow in the bottom-right corner of the **Paragraph** group under the **Home** tab).

c. Under the **Indents and Spacing** tab, select **First line** from the **Special** dropdown and set the desired measurement.

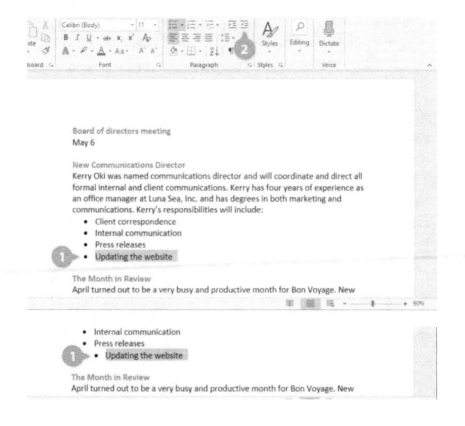

2. **Hanging Indent**
   - Often used in bibliographies or references, where the first line remains at the margin, and subsequent lines are indented.

- How to apply:
  a. Highlight the paragraph.
  b. Open the **Paragraph** dialog box.
  c. From the **Special** dropdown, choose **Hanging** and adjust the measurement.

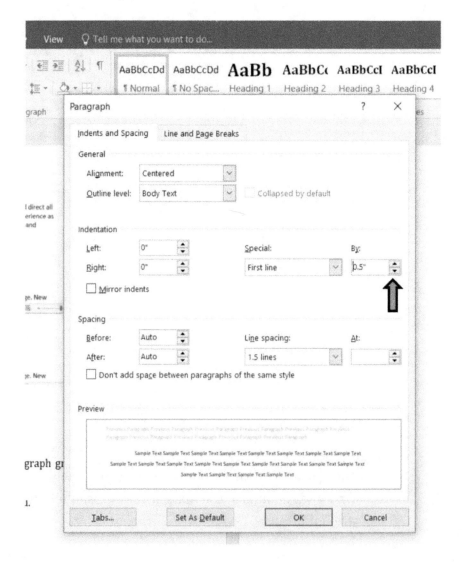

3. **Left and Right Indents**
    - ○ Entire paragraphs can also be indented from the left or right margins to create distinct sections or quotes.
    - ○ **How to apply**: Drag the indent markers on the ruler or adjust the **Left** and **Right** fields in the **Paragraph** dialog box.

Pro Tip: You can use the **Tab** key to quickly add a first-line indent while typing.

Managing Line and Paragraph Spacing: Maintaining Readability

Proper spacing between lines and paragraphs ensures that your document is easy to read and visually appealing.

1. **Line Spacing**
    - ○ Line spacing refers to the vertical space between lines in a paragraph. Common options include single, 1.5, or double spacing.
    - ○ **How to adjust**:
      a. Select the paragraph.
      b. In the **Home** tab, click the **Line and Paragraph Spacing** button (icon with up-and-down arrows).
      c. Choose from the preset options, or click **Line Spacing Options** for custom settings.

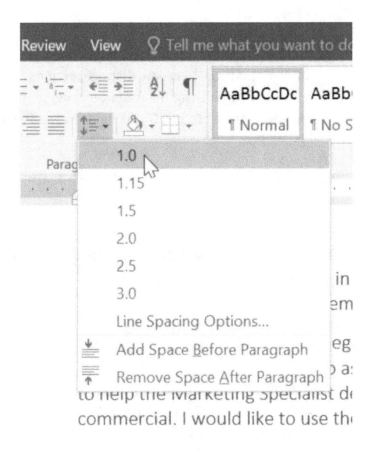

commercial. I would like to use the

2. **Paragraph Spacing**
   o You can also add extra space before or after paragraphs to create clear separations between sections.
   o **How to adjust**:
   a. Select the paragraph.
   b. Open the **Paragraph** dialog box.
   c. Under **Spacing**, adjust the values for **Before** and **After**.
3. **Using Presets for Spacing**

- Word offers pre-designed styles for line and paragraph spacing. You can find these under the **Design** tab in the **Document Formatting** group.

Example: Use 1.15 line spacing and 10pt paragraph spacing after body text for a professional look.

Creating Bulleted and Numbered Lists

Lists are an excellent way to organize information clearly. Microsoft Word provides tools for creating both bulleted and numbered lists.

1. **Bulleted Lists**
   - Perfect for items that don't follow a sequence, such as grocery lists or brainstorming ideas.
   - **How to create**:
     a. Highlight the items you want to turn into a list.
     b. Click the **Bullets** button in the **Home** tab.
     c. Choose from the default bullet styles or click **Define New Bullet** for custom symbols.

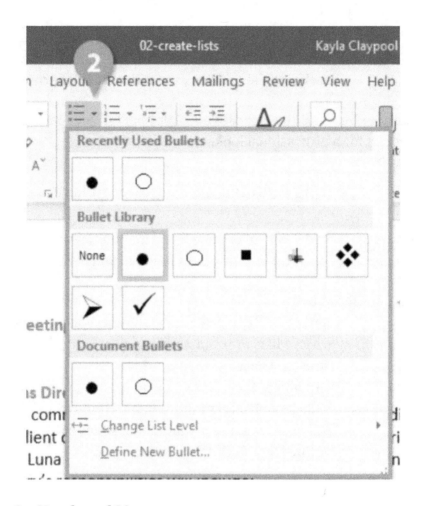

2. **Numbered Lists**
   - Use numbered lists when the order of items matters, such as step-by-step instructions.
   - **How to create:**
     a. Highlight your text.
     b. Click the **Numbering** button in the **Home** tab.
     c. Select a numbering style, or customize it by choosing **Define New Number Format**.

Numbering Library

None

1. ⎯⎯⎯
2. ⎯⎯⎯
3. ⎯⎯⎯

1) ⎯⎯⎯
2) ⎯⎯⎯
3) ⎯⎯⎯

I. ⎯⎯⎯
II. ⎯⎯⎯
III. ⎯⎯⎯

A. ⎯⎯⎯
B. ⎯⎯⎯
C. ⎯⎯⎯

a) ⎯⎯⎯
b) ⎯⎯⎯
c) ⎯⎯⎯

a. ⎯⎯⎯
b. ⎯⎯⎯
c. ⎯⎯⎯

i. ⎯⎯⎯
ii. ⎯⎯⎯
iii. ⎯⎯⎯

Change List Level   >

Define New Number Format...

3. **Multilevel Lists**
   - For complex hierarchies or subcategories, use multilevel lists.
   - **How to create**:
     a. Click the **Multilevel List** button in the **Home** tab.
     b. Choose a style or create a custom structure by clicking **Define New Multilevel List**.
4. **Customizing Lists**

o To adjust the appearance of your list:
a. Right-click a bullet or number and select **Adjust List Indents**.
b. Use the **Font** dialog box to change the size or color of bullets and numbers.

Pro Tip: Use lists sparingly in formal documents to maintain a clean and professional appearance.

Quick Tips for Professional Paragraph Formatting

- Use consistent alignment throughout your document to avoid a cluttered look.
- Opt for **single-line spacing** for resumes and **double-line spacing** for academic papers.
- Combine bullets with hanging indents for well-organized lists.
- Save custom spacing settings as a style for quick application to future documents.

Mastering paragraph formatting in Word is essential for creating clean, visually appealing documents. With these tools at your disposal, you can ensure your content is both reader-friendly and professional. Take the time to experiment with these features to see how small adjustments can make a big difference!

Chapter 10: Mastering Page Layout and Design

When working on a document, its layout and design are just as crucial as its content. A well-organized layout enhances readability, professionalism, and visual appeal. In this chapter, we'll dive into the tools and features that allow you to control the structure of your pages, from adjusting margins to using headers and footers effectively. By the end of this section, you'll have a polished, well-designed document ready for any audience.

1. Adjusting Margins

Margins are the blank spaces around the edges of your page. They play a significant role in determining how your content fits on the page. Microsoft Word makes it easy to adjust margins for a consistent and professional appearance.

Steps to Adjust Margins:

1. Navigate to the **Layout** tab on the Ribbon.
2. Click on **Margins** in the **Page Setup** group.
3. Select from predefined options such as **Normal, Narrow, Moderate,** or **Wide**.

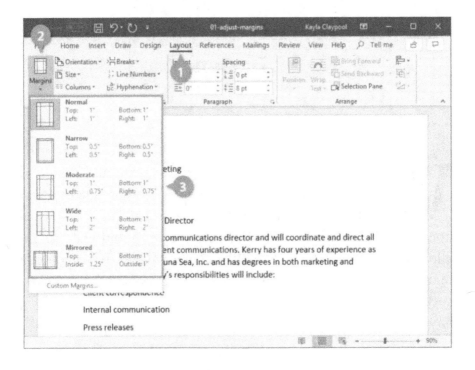

4. If none of these meet your needs, choose **Custom Margins** at the bottom of the list.

   o In the **Page Setup** dialog box, enter specific measurements for the **Top**, **Bottom**, **Left**, and **Right** margins.

   o Preview the changes in the sample display area and click **OK** to apply.

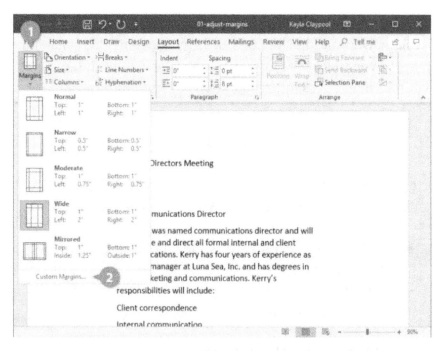

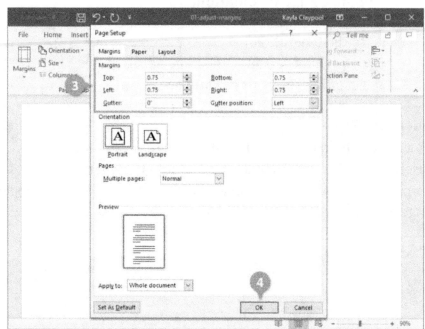

Pro Tip:
Use narrower margins for content-heavy documents to maximize space, but opt for wider margins when preparing printed materials like letters or presentations to maintain a clean look.

2. Changing Page Orientation

Orientation determines the direction in which your content is displayed on the page. Microsoft Word offers two options:

- **Portrait** (vertical layout) – Ideal for text-heavy documents like letters and reports.
- **Landscape** (horizontal layout) – Suitable for wide tables, charts, or design-heavy documents.

Steps to Change Page Orientation:

1. Go to the **Layout** tab.
2. Click on **Orientation** in the **Page Setup** group.
3. Select either **Portrait** or **Landscape**.

Advanced Tip:
You can use both orientations within the same document by inserting section breaks (discussed later in this chapter). This is helpful when you want to display a wide table or chart on a single page without affecting the rest of the document.

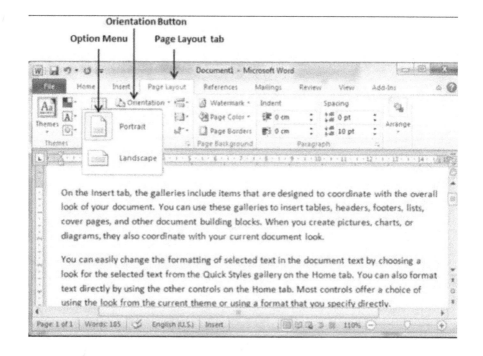

On the Insert tab, the galleries include items that are designed to coordinate with the overall look of your document. You can use these galleries to insert tables, headers, footers, lists, cover pages, and other document building blocks. When you create pictures, charts, or diagrams, they also coordinate with your current document look.

You can easily change the formatting of selected text in the document text by choosing a look for the selected text from the Quick Styles gallery on the Home tab. You can also format text directly by using the other controls on the Home tab. Most controls offer a choice of using the look from the current theme or using a format that you specify directly.

3. Adjusting Page Size

Word provides several predefined page sizes and allows you to customize the dimensions for unique needs like brochures or posters.

Steps to Adjust Page Size:

1. Go to the **Layout** tab.
2. Click **Size** in the **Page Setup** group.
3. Choose from standard sizes such as **Letter**, **A4**, **Legal**, or others.
4. For custom sizes, click **More Paper Sizes** at the bottom of the list.

o Enter specific dimensions for the **Width** and **Height** in the dialog box.

o Confirm your selection by clicking **OK**.

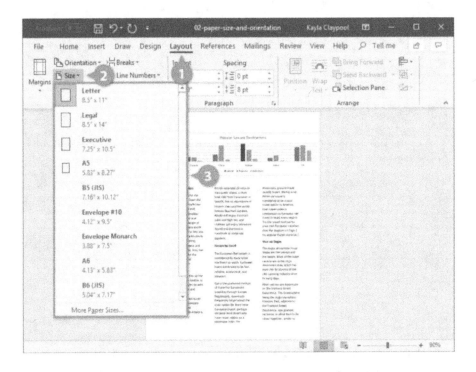

Practical Application:

- Use **Letter (8.5" x 11")** for most U.S. documents.
- Opt for **A4 (8.27" x 11.69")** for international documents.
- Adjust custom sizes for special projects like flyers or posters.

4. Setting Up Headers and Footers

Headers and footers are essential for adding consistent information, such as document titles, page numbers, and dates, across multiple pages.

Steps to Add a Header or Footer:

1. Go to the **Insert** tab on the Ribbon.

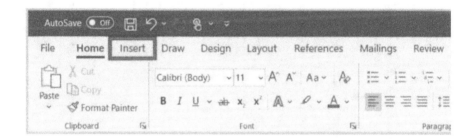

2. Click on **Header** or **Footer** in the **Header & Footer** group.
3. Choose a pre-designed option or select **Edit Header/Footer** for a custom layout.

4. Add the desired text, such as your name, document title, or company logo.
5. Use the tools in the **Header & Footer Tools Design** tab to customize the alignment, font, or style.

Quick Customization Tips:

- Check the **Different First Page** option if you want a unique header or footer on the first page.
- Use the **Different Odd & Even Pages** option to create alternating headers or footers for books or reports.

5. Adding Page Numbers

Page numbers help readers navigate your document efficiently, especially when dealing with multi-page content.

Steps to Insert Page Numbers:

1. Go to the **Insert** tab.

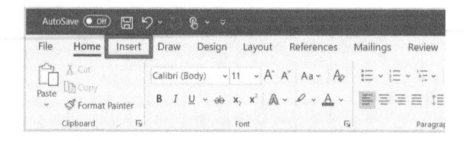

2. Click on **Page Number** in the **Header & Footer** group.
3. Select the location:
   - **Top of Page**
   - **Bottom of Page**
   - **Page Margins**
   - **Current Position** (where your cursor is placed).

4. Choose a style, such as plain numbers or numbers with embellishments.

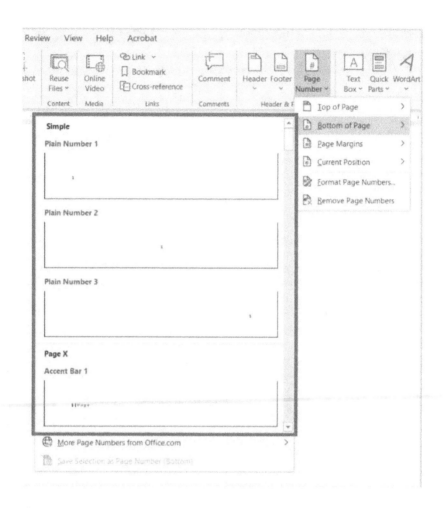

Customizing Page Numbers:

- To start numbering from a specific page, use section breaks and adjust the numbering in the **Format Page Numbers** dialog box.
- Combine headers/footers with page numbers for a professional touch.

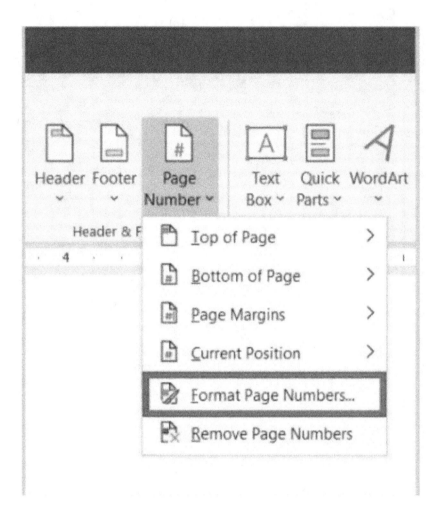

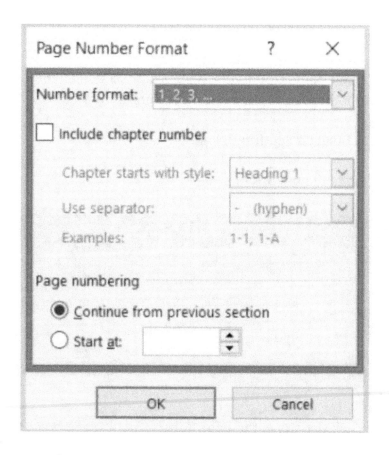

6. Working with Section Breaks

Section breaks allow you to divide your document into distinct parts with unique formatting. This is particularly useful for applying different page layouts or numbering styles within the same document.

Types of Section Breaks:

- **Next Page**: Starts a new section on the next page.

- **Continuous**: Begins a new section on the same page, useful for multi-column layouts.
- **Even Page/Odd Page**: Starts a new section on the next even or odd page, often used in booklets.

Steps to Insert a Section Break:

1. Go to the **Layout** tab.

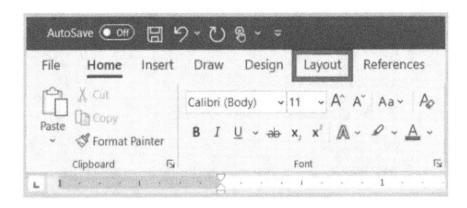

2. Click **Breaks** in the **Page Setup** group.

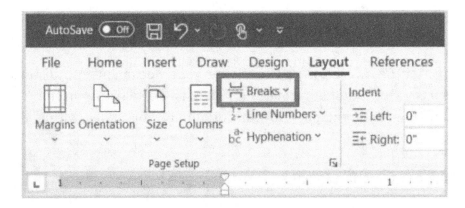

3. Choose the desired section break type.

Common Use Cases:

- Different headers/footers for chapters in a book.
- Alternating page orientations in one document.

7. Using Page Breaks

Page breaks are used to control the flow of your content by forcing text to start on a new page. Unlike section breaks, they don't affect formatting.

Steps to Insert a Page Break:

1. Place your cursor where you want the new page to begin.
2. Press **Ctrl+Enter** or go to the **Insert** tab and select **Page Break**.

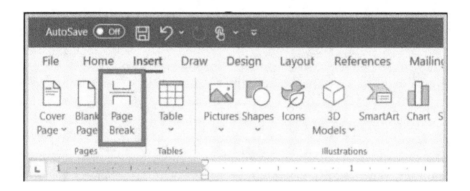

Practical Applications:

- Ensure chapters in a report or book begin on a new page.
- Separate content visually for better readability.

Tips for Effective Page Layout Design

1. **Consistency is Key**: Maintain uniform margins, font styles, and spacing throughout the document for a polished look.

2. **Test Your Layout**: Use **Print Preview** to see how your document will appear on paper.
3. **Avoid Overcrowding**: Leave enough white space for a clean and professional appearance.
4. **Experiment with Templates**: Use Word's pre-designed templates as a starting point for complex projects like reports or brochures.

By mastering these layout and design tools, you'll have full control over how your documents look and feel. Whether you're working on a resume, a school project, or a professional report, these techniques will help you create visually appealing and highly functional documents.

Chapter 11: Working with Tables in Microsoft Word

Tables are essential tools in Microsoft Word for organizing and presenting data in a structured way. Whether you're designing a report, creating schedules, or displaying lists, Word makes it easy to create and manipulate tables to suit your needs. This chapter will guide you through the process of creating, editing, and formatting tables for a professional look.

Creating a Table from Scratch

Creating a table in Microsoft Word is a simple process, but it can make a significant difference in how your information is presented. Follow these steps to add a table to your document:

1. **Insert a Table**:
   - Navigate to the **Insert** tab on the Ribbon.
   - In the **Tables** group, click the **Table** button. A grid will appear showing rows and columns.

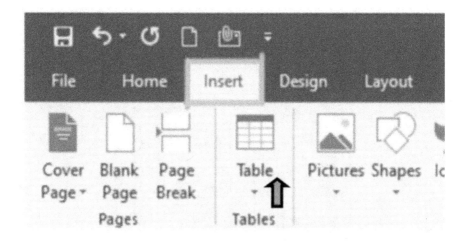

- o Hover over the grid to highlight the number of rows and columns you need. For example, if you want a 3x4 table, hover to select 3 rows and 4 columns.

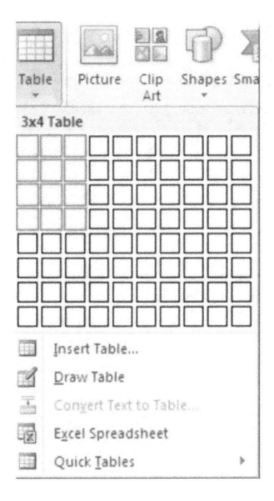

- o Click to insert the table into your document.
2. **Using the Insert Table Dialog Box**:
    - o Alternatively, click on the **Insert Table** option (found in the **Table** menu).
    - o A dialog box will appear where you can specify the exact number of rows and columns you need.
    - o After entering your desired row and column count, click **OK** to insert the table.

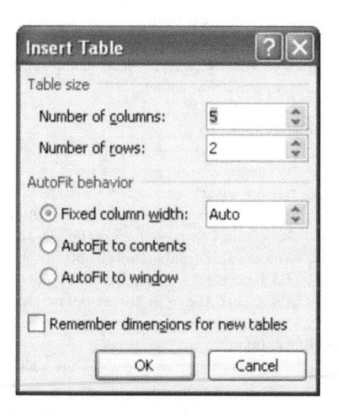

3. **Drawing a Table**:
   - If you want more flexibility with your table's design, you can draw it manually. Under the **Insert** tab, choose **Table** and then select **Draw Table**.
   - This will change the cursor to a pencil icon, allowing you to click and drag to draw the structure of your table.

Adding and Removing Rows/Columns

Once your table is inserted, you can easily modify its structure by adding or removing rows and columns.

1. **Adding Rows**:
    - To add a row, right-click on the table where you want the new row to appear.
    - Choose **Insert** from the context menu, then select **Insert Rows Above** or **Insert Rows Below** depending on where you want the row to appear.
    - You can also use the **Table Tools** that appear when the table is selected. Under the **Layout** tab, click on the **Insert Above** or **Insert Below** buttons in the Rows & Columns group.
2. **Adding Columns**:
    - To add a column, right-click on the table where you want the new column to appear.
    - Choose **Insert** from the context menu, then select **Insert Columns to the Left** or **Insert Columns to the Right**.

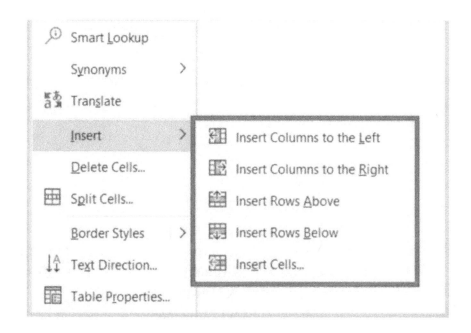

- o Alternatively, use the **Table Tools Layout** tab and click on the **Insert Left** or **Insert Right** options to add columns.

3. **Removing Rows or Columns**:
    - o To remove a row, right-click on the row number on the left side of the table and select **Delete Rows** from the context menu.
    - o To remove a column, right-click on the column number at the top of the table and select **Delete Columns**.
    - o You can also remove rows or columns using the **Table Tools Layout** tab. Simply click **Delete** and choose whether to delete rows, columns, or the entire table.

Merging and Splitting Cells

Microsoft Word allows you to combine multiple cells into one larger cell or divide a single cell into smaller ones, giving you greater control over the structure of your table.

1. **Merging Cells**:
    - To merge two or more cells, first select the cells you want to combine. Click and drag across the cells or hold down the **Ctrl** key to select multiple cells.
    - Right-click on the selected cells and choose **Merge Cells** from the context menu, or go to the **Table Tools Layout** tab and click **Merge Cells** in the Merge group.
    - The selected cells will now combine into one larger cell. This is particularly useful for creating header cells or for spanning text across several columns.

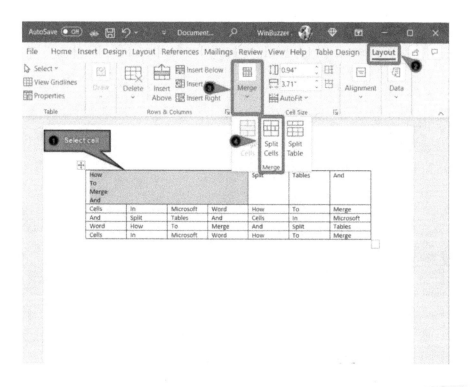

2. **Splitting Cells**:
   - To split a cell into multiple smaller cells, first select the cell you want to split.
   - Right-click and choose **Split Cells** from the context menu, or go to the **Table Tools Layout** tab and click **Split Cells** in the Merge group.
   - A dialog box will appear where you can specify how many rows and columns you want the cell to be split into. For example, you can split a single cell into two columns and two rows.

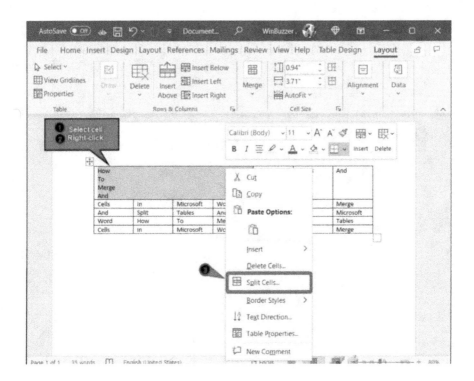

Applying Table Styles for a Professional Look

Tables in Microsoft Word can be customized to fit the style and design of your document. Word offers a variety of pre-designed table styles, but you can also create your own to ensure consistency across your documents.

1. **Using Pre-designed Table Styles**:
   - After selecting your table, go to the **Table Tools Design** tab on the Ribbon.
   - In the **Table Styles** group, you'll see a variety of predefined styles. These styles include different color schemes, borders, and shading options.

- o Hover over each style to preview how it will look on your table, then click to apply the style.
- o If you want to customize the style further, you can change the colors, borders, and shading by selecting options from the **Shading** and **Borders** menus within the **Design** tab.

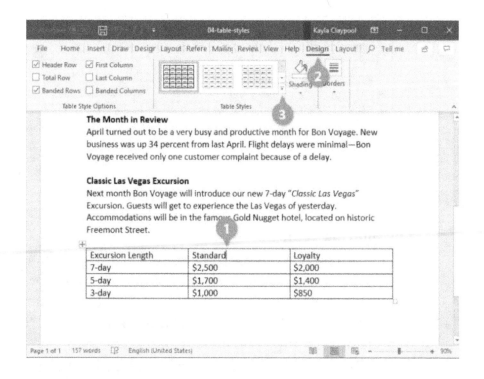

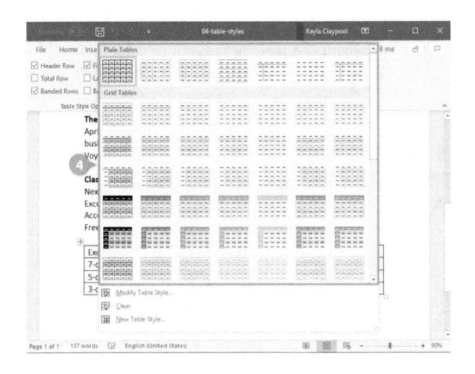

2. **Customizing Table Borders**:
   - To modify the borders of your table, click on the table to select it, then go to the **Table Tools Design** tab.
   - In the **Borders** group, you can choose from options such as **All Borders**, **Outside Borders**, or **No Borders**.
   - To manually adjust individual borders, click **Borders and Shading** from the drop-down menu, where you can select specific borders for individual cells, rows, or columns.

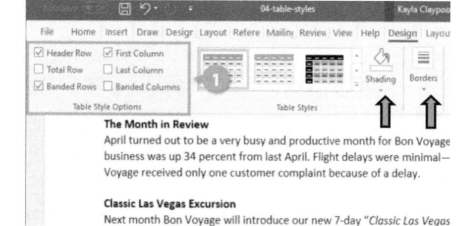

The Month in Review

April turned out to be a very busy and productive month for Bon Voyage business was up 34 percent from last April. Flight delays were minimal— Voyage received only one customer complaint because of a delay.

Classic Las Vegas Excursion

Next month Bon Voyage will introduce our new 7-day "*Classic Las Vegas*

3. **Shading and Color**:
    - In the **Table Tools Design** tab, you can add color to the cells to make them stand out or match the document's theme.
    - Click on **Shading** and choose a color from the palette. You can apply shading to specific cells, rows, or columns.
    - To create a gradient or more complex effects, click **Borders and Shading** and explore the additional options.

4. **Adjusting Table Layout**:
    - You can change the overall layout of your table by modifying its size, spacing, and alignment.
    - In the **Table Tools Layout** tab, you can adjust cell size, distribute rows and columns evenly, and set specific dimensions for your cells.
    - For better control, use the **AutoFit** option to automatically adjust the table's size to fit the content,

or select **Fixed Column Width** for more precise control over column dimensions.

Using Tables for Advanced Layouts

Once you become comfortable with basic table creation and formatting, you can use tables to create more complex layouts in your documents. For example, tables can be used to:

- **Design newsletters or brochures**: Use tables for sections like headings, text, and images, ensuring a uniform and professional layout.
- **Create schedules or calendars**: Organize data in a grid format for events, dates, or appointments.
- **Align complex content**: When working with multi-column layouts, tables can help organize text and graphics without the need for complex formatting.

Conclusion

Tables are one of the most powerful features in Microsoft Word, enabling you to display data in a structured and visually appealing way. From inserting a table to customizing its layout and design, Microsoft Word provides a wealth of tools to help you make your tables both functional and attractive.

By mastering tables, you'll be able to create professional documents, presentations, and reports with ease. Keep experimenting with different table styles and configurations to find the best layout for your content. The flexibility and power of tables in Word are vast, and the more you use them, the more efficient and polished your documents will become.

Chapter 12: Adding Visual Elements

When it comes to creating professional and visually engaging documents in Microsoft Word, adding visual elements like pictures, shapes, icons, and SmartArt is essential. These elements help communicate your message more effectively, break up blocks of text, and add a touch of creativity. This chapter will guide you through the process of incorporating various visual elements into your documents, ensuring that you can enhance the appearance and functionality of your work.

Inserting Pictures and Online Images

One of the most commonly used visual elements in any document is **pictures**. Whether you're adding a photo, a logo, or an infographic, Microsoft Word allows you to insert images from different sources. Here's how you can do it:

1. **Inserting a Picture from Your Computer**:
   - Go to the **Insert** tab on the Ribbon.
   - Click on **Pictures** in the **Illustrations** group. A menu will appear offering you two options:
     - **This Device**: Choose this option if you want to insert an image from your computer.

- **Online Pictures**: This allows you to search for images from the web, including free stock images, from sources like Bing, or OneDrive if you're signed in to your Microsoft account.

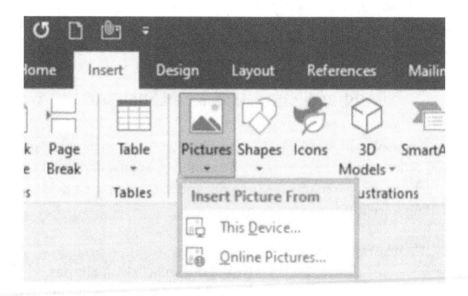

- After selecting your image, click **Insert**, and the picture will be placed into your document.

The inserted image will appear where your cursor is located, and you can then adjust it as needed.

2. **Inserting a Picture from Online Sources**:
   - If you're inserting an image from an online source, simply type in a keyword in the search box under **Online Pictures** and hit enter. Word will show a list of results from various online image repositories.

- Select the image you wish to use, click on it, and then click **Insert**. This can save you time when looking for visuals that match your content.

After inserting an image, Microsoft Word allows you to adjust its layout, size, and alignment, so it fits perfectly within your document's design.

Adding Shapes, Icons, and SmartArt

Microsoft Word doesn't just stop at images—it also allows you to add other graphic elements, such as **shapes**, **icons**, and **SmartArt**, which can be helpful for creating diagrams, emphasizing points, or adding a creative touch.

1. **Inserting Shapes**:
   - Navigate to the **Insert** tab and click on **Shapes**.
   - You'll find a wide selection of shapes, including basic shapes like circles, rectangles, and lines, as well as more complex ones like arrows, flowcharts, stars, and callouts.

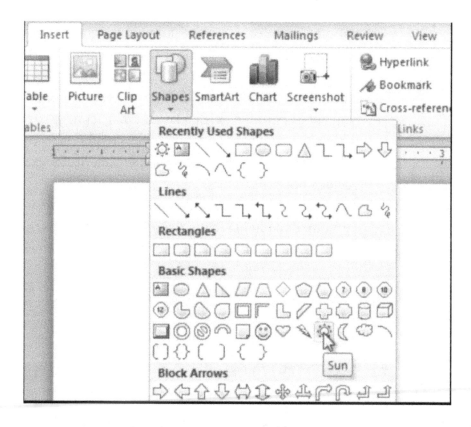

- o Once you select a shape, your cursor will change into a crosshair. Click and drag on your document to draw the shape. You can adjust its size later by dragging the corners or edges.

Customizing Shapes:

- o After drawing a shape, you can modify its color, outline, and effects. Click on the shape to select it, and the **Shape Format** tab will appear in the Ribbon. Here, you can choose from various formatting options, such as filling the shape with color, adding gradient effects, or changing the border width.

2. **Inserting Icons**:

   o Icons are simple graphics that can symbolize concepts, actions, or ideas. To insert an icon, go to the **Insert** tab, click **Icons**, and search for the icon that fits your needs (such as arrows, social media icons, or various objects).

   o Once selected, click **Insert**, and the icon will appear on your document. Icons are vector-based, so they can be resized without losing quality.

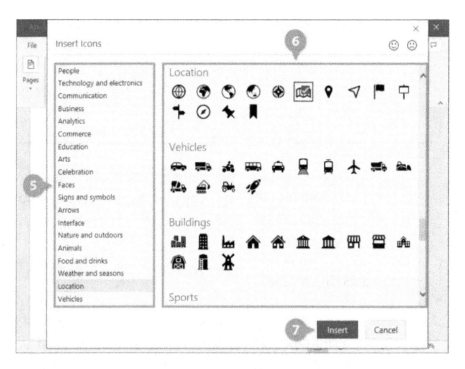

Customizing Icons:

- o After inserting the icon, you can change its color, size, and rotation by selecting the icon and using the options in the **Graphics Format** tab.

3. **Inserting SmartArt:**

- o SmartArt is a feature that lets you create visually appealing diagrams like lists, processes, hierarchies, and cycles. To insert SmartArt, go to the **Insert** tab, click on **SmartArt**, and choose from various graphic types.

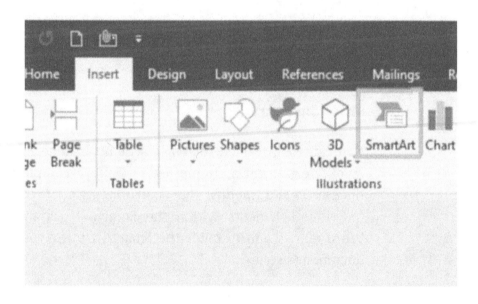

- o Once you've selected your SmartArt, a new window will appear, allowing you to enter your text into the diagram. You can also change the layout and colors of the SmartArt graphic using the **SmartArt Tools** in the Ribbon.

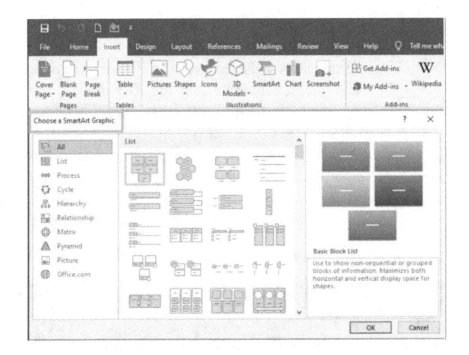

Customizing SmartArt:

- o You can easily adjust the color scheme, change the layout (e.g., from a simple list to a more complex diagram), and modify the size and style of the individual elements within the SmartArt graphic. Word allows you to tailor the SmartArt to fit your document's style.

Formatting and Resizing Images

Once you've inserted your image or visual element, it's important to adjust its size and position for optimal viewing. Word provides several tools for this:

1. **Resizing Images**:
   o Select the image by clicking on it. Small circles or squares (called **resize handles**) will appear on the edges and corners of the image.
   o To resize, click and drag these handles. Dragging from the corners will keep the image's proportions intact, while dragging from the sides or top/bottom will distort the proportions.

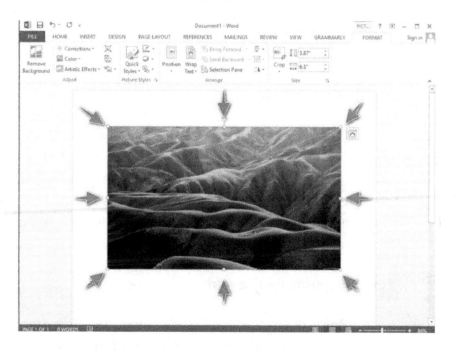

Quick Resize:

   o Alternatively, you can use the **Picture Tools** in the Ribbon under the **Format** tab to set the exact dimensions of your image. This ensures your image is resized to the precise measurements you need.
2. **Positioning Images**:

- Word allows you to adjust the position of an image within the text to create a more polished layout. Once the image is selected, you'll see a small icon called **Layout Options** next to it. Click this icon to choose how the image interacts with the text.
- **Text Wrapping**: The Layout Options menu offers various wrapping styles, such as **In Line with Text**, **Square**, **Tight**, **Through**, and **Behind Text**. The most commonly used option is **Square**, which allows text to flow around the image smoothly. You can also select **Tight** for even closer wrapping.

Positioning for Alignment:

- If you want to center your image or align it with the text in a specific way, you can use the **Align** tool in the **Format** tab under **Picture Tools**. Here, you can align your image to the left, center, or right, as well as adjust its distance from the page's edges or other elements.

Text Wrapping and Layout:

- **Behind Text**: If you need to layer an image behind the text (for example, a watermark or a decorative background image), select the **Behind Text** option from the Layout Options menu.
- **In Front of Text**: Similarly, if you want the image to sit on top of the text, choose **In Front of Text**.
- **Custom Layouts**: You can create more complex layouts by manually adjusting the image and text

placement. Word lets you click and drag the image to any position, even within tables or text boxes.

Using Text Wrapping for Better Layout

Text wrapping is a vital feature when you're integrating visual elements into your document. It allows you to control how text flows around an image, shape, or other graphic elements, giving you full control over your document's layout. Here are a few key options for wrapping text:

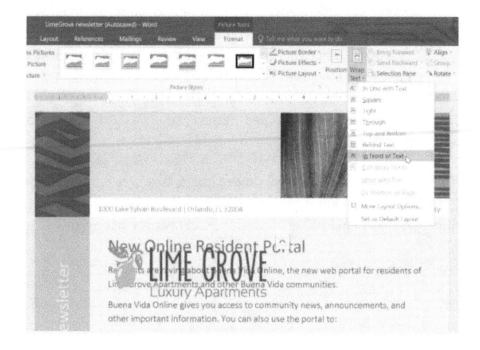

1. **In Line with Text**: The default setting, where the image or graphic is treated as if it were a block of text. The image will move up or down along with the text as you type.

2. **Square**: This option wraps text around the image in a square pattern, giving your document a clean and neat look. It's ideal for smaller images, allowing text to flow smoothly along the edges.

3. **Tight**: This setting creates an even closer wrap around your image, following the contours of the object. It works well for irregularly shaped images, ensuring the text conforms more closely to the graphic.

4. **Behind Text**: With this option, the image is placed in the background, allowing the text to flow in front of it. This is ideal for watermarks or background images that you don't want to interfere with the readability of your document.

5. **In Front of Text**: If you want the image to appear on top of the text, select this option. It's often used for decorative images, like logos or captions.

6. **Through**: This is a more complex setting that wraps text in a very tight and detailed pattern, often used when there's intricate graphic design involved.

To apply text wrapping, click on the image to select it, then choose your desired wrapping style from the **Layout Options** button that appears. This helps you achieve the exact layout you envision.

Chapter 13: Templates and Styles

Templates and styles are two powerful features in Microsoft Word that can help you save time, maintain consistency, and enhance the overall look of your documents. In this chapter, we'll dive into how to explore pre-designed templates, create custom templates tailored to your needs, and apply and modify styles to ensure your documents have a professional appearance.

Exploring Pre-Designed Templates

Microsoft Word comes with a wide selection of pre-designed templates that can make creating professional-looking documents quick and easy. Whether you need to create a resume, letter, report, or invitation, Word's templates are a great starting point.

What Are Templates?

A template in Word is essentially a predefined layout that includes formatting, design, and even text placeholders. It is designed to help you quickly create documents without needing to start from scratch. Templates come in various categories such as:

- **Business**: These include professional documents such as letters, reports, and proposals.

- **Resumes and Cover Letters**: Various formats and styles to help you create job application documents.
- **Reports**: Pre-arranged formats for creating academic or professional reports, complete with headings, sections, and formatting.
- **Newsletters**: Ready-to-use designs for newsletter layouts, often incorporating images, text boxes, and columns.
- **Calendars and Planners**: Templates for scheduling, event planning, and yearly calendars.

How to Access Pre-Designed Templates:

1. Open Microsoft Word and click on **File** in the upper left corner.
2. Select **New** to open the templates gallery.
3. You'll be presented with a range of categories. You can either:
   - Browse through the recommended templates.
   - Use the **Search** bar to type in the type of document you want (e.g., "Resume", "Invoice", "Agenda").
4. Select the template you want to use and click **Create**.

Once the template is opened, you can begin filling in your information. Templates can include sample text that you can replace with your content. For example, a resume template may have pre-written headings such as "Experience," "Education," and "Skills," which you can simply update with your personal information.

Customizing Templates:

Although templates are pre-designed, you're not locked into the original design. You can modify the template to suit your needs. You can change the fonts, colors, layout, and any other design elements.

1. Click on any section of the template and begin editing it.
2. You can adjust font styles and sizes, change the color scheme, and add or remove elements as you wish.

Templates can be a fantastic way to save time while ensuring your document follows a professional format.

Creating and Saving Custom Templates

While Word provides a variety of built-in templates, you may want to create your own template to use for similar documents in the future. Creating a custom template is an excellent way to maintain consistency across your documents, especially if you have a specific format or style you prefer.

Why Create a Custom Template?

- **Consistency**: Templates ensure that all of your documents have the same structure, font choices, spacing, and other formatting, making your work look polished and professional.
- **Efficiency**: Instead of formatting each document from scratch, you can start with a template that already has your desired design, layout, and settings.

How to Create a Custom Template:

1. **Start with a Blank Document**: Open a new blank document by going to **File > New > Blank Document**.
2. **Design Your Layout**: Set up the layout and design elements according to your preferences. This could include:
   o Choosing a font style and size for headings, subheadings, and body text.
   o Adjusting the page margins and orientation (portrait or landscape).
   o Inserting headers and footers, and deciding whether to include page numbers.
   o Adding your logo or other images, if desired.
3. **Save Your Document as a Template**:
   o Once you're happy with the design, go to **File > Save As**.
   o In the **Save as Type** dropdown menu, select **Word Template** (*.dotx).
   o Choose a location on your computer (or cloud storage) to save the template.
   o Give your template a meaningful name so you can easily find it later (e.g., "Company Letterhead Template" or "Project Report Template").
4. **Use Your Custom Template**:
   o The next time you need to create a document with this layout, go to **File > New** and click **Personal** or **Custom** (depending on your version of Word).
   o Your custom template will appear under **My Templates**. Select it and click **Create** to start working with your personalized design.

Now, instead of manually setting up each document, you can simply use your custom template as a starting point.

Applying and Modifying Styles

Styles in Word are predefined sets of formatting options that control the appearance of text, headings, and paragraphs. By applying styles, you can quickly format your document with consistent fonts, sizes, colors, and spacing. Word provides a variety of built-in styles, but you can also create your own to meet your specific needs.

What Are Styles?

Styles allow you to apply a set of formatting options—such as font type, size, color, and paragraph alignment—to different sections of your document. Styles are particularly useful when working with long documents as they help you maintain uniform formatting throughout. Common types of styles include:

- **Heading Styles**: These styles are typically used for section titles or chapter headings. They make it easy to organize your document into different sections, making it more readable and professional.
- **Paragraph Styles**: Used for formatting the main body of your text. They can be customized for alignment, indentation, line spacing, etc.
- **List Styles**: These are used for creating bulleted or numbered lists, allowing you to apply consistent formatting to all items in the list.

How to Apply a Style:

1. Select the text you want to format (heading, body text, etc.).
2. On the **Home** tab, locate the **Styles** section.
3. Click on a style that you want to apply. The style will instantly change the appearance of the selected text according to the predefined settings.

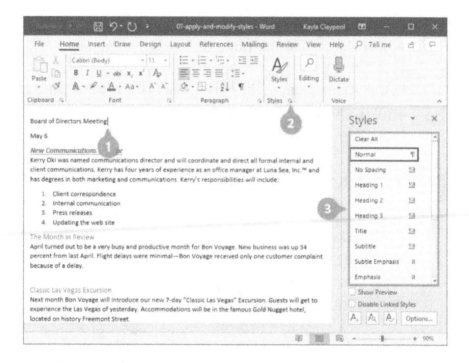

Modifying a Style:

If the built-in styles don't fit your needs, you can modify them:

1. Right-click on the style you want to modify in the **Styles** section.
2. Select **Modify**.

3. A dialog box will appear allowing you to change various settings such as font, size, color, alignment, and spacing.
4. After making your changes, click **OK**. The style will be updated, and any text in the document using that style will be automatically updated to match the new formatting.

Creating a Custom Style:

1. Highlight the text you want to format.
2. Adjust the formatting (font, size, color, alignment, etc.) to your liking.
3. In the **Styles** section, click the **More** button (the downward arrow) and select **Create a Style**.
4. Name your style and click **OK**.

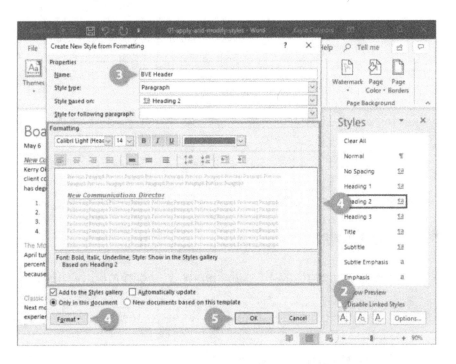

Now, you can apply your custom style to any section of your document simply by selecting it from the **Styles** section.

Using Styles for Table of Contents:

One of the most powerful uses of styles is generating a **Table of Contents** (TOC). Since heading styles are used to define sections of your document, Word can automatically generate a TOC based on those heading styles.

1. Apply heading styles to your section titles.
2. Place the cursor where you want the TOC to appear.
3. Go to the **References** tab and click **Table of Contents**.
4. Choose a style, and Word will generate the TOC based on the headings in your document.

This feature saves you a lot of time, especially when working with long documents, as it updates automatically when you add or remove headings.

Conclusion

Templates and styles in Microsoft Word are incredibly useful tools for anyone looking to create documents with a consistent, professional appearance. Templates allow you to quickly create structured documents, while styles help maintain formatting consistency throughout your work. By mastering both, you can improve your productivity and ensure your documents look polished, every time. Whether you're working on business reports, school assignments, or personal projects, templates and styles will be your best allies in creating high-quality content in Microsoft Word.

Chapter 14: Using Word for Collaboration

Collaboration is a vital part of working with others on a document, whether it's for business, school, or personal projects. Microsoft Word has powerful features that facilitate teamwork, allowing multiple people to work on the same document simultaneously or at different times. In this chapter, we'll dive into the tools available for effective collaboration, including adding and managing comments, using Track Changes for edits, and sharing documents for real-time collaboration.

1. Adding and Managing Comments

One of the most common ways to collaborate on a document is through comments. Comments allow reviewers or collaborators to provide feedback without altering the content of the document. This is particularly useful in situations where you might be drafting a report, writing a paper, or editing a document that others need to review.

How to Add a Comment

To add a comment, follow these steps:

1. **Select the Text**: Highlight the text or place the cursor where you want to add a comment. This could be a section of text that needs clarification, a suggestion, or a question.
2. **Insert a Comment**:
   - Go to the **Review** tab in the Ribbon.
   - In the **Comments** group, click on **New Comment**.
   - A comment box will appear on the right side of the document, where you can type your message or feedback.
3. **Typing the Comment**: Enter the details of the comment in the box. You can explain what needs to be changed, ask a question, or leave notes for the writer.

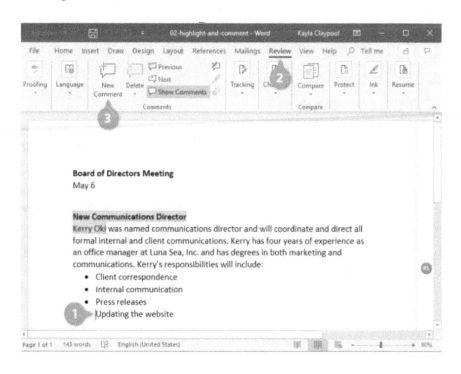

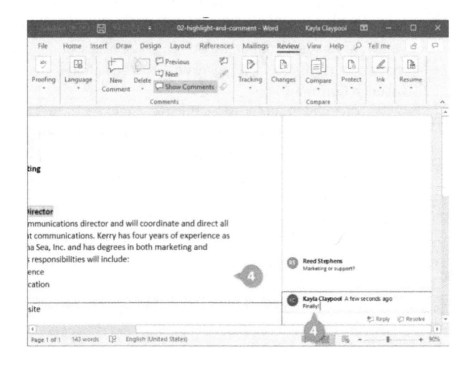

Managing Comments

Once comments are added, Word provides several tools for managing them effectively:

- **Replying to Comments**: If you're reviewing the document and want to respond to a comment, you can click on the comment and select **Reply**. This helps keep the conversation going within the context of the comment.

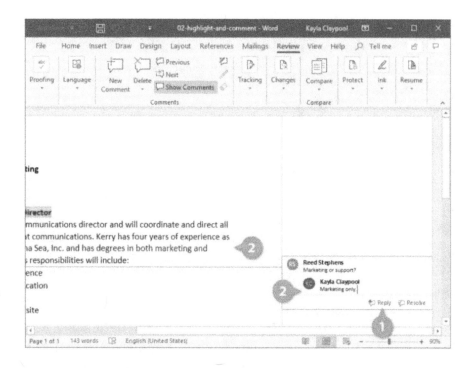

- **Navigating Through Comments**: If there are many comments in a document, you can easily navigate between them by clicking the **Next** and **Previous** buttons in the **Comments** section of the **Review** tab.

- **Deleting Comments**: To remove a comment once it has been addressed, right-click on the comment box and select **Delete Comment**, or go to the **Review** tab and click **Delete**. You can choose to delete individual comments or remove all comments in the document at once.
- **Marking Comments as Done**: You can mark comments as resolved when you feel the issue has been addressed. Right-click on the comment and select **Mark as Done**. This doesn't delete the comment but shows it as completed.

Adding and managing comments helps keep the document organized while allowing the document's authors and collaborators to easily track feedback and revisions.

2. Using Track Changes for Edits

Another essential tool for collaboration in Word is **Track Changes**. This feature allows you to see every change made to the document, whether it's text additions, deletions, or formatting modifications. It's incredibly useful for editing, as it lets you track who made which changes and when, making it easy to review and accept or reject those changes.

Turning On Track Changes

To begin tracking changes, follow these steps:

1. **Activate Track Changes**:
   o Go to the **Review** tab.
   o In the **Tracking** group, click on the **Track Changes** button to turn on the feature.
   o Once activated, any changes you make to the document will be highlighted, and Word will keep a record of these changes.

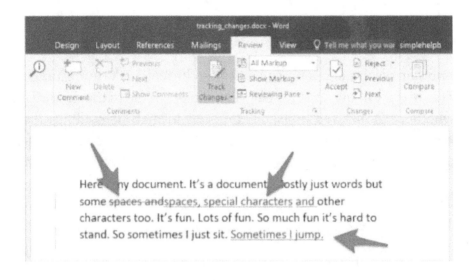

2. **Adjusting Track Changes Settings**:
   o By default, Track Changes will highlight insertions, deletions, and formatting changes with different colors.
   o If you want to customize the way changes are displayed (for instance, choosing whether to show deletions in a strikethrough or hidden text format), click on the small arrow next to the **Track Changes** button and select **Track Changes Options**.

Making Changes and Reviewing Edits

Once Track Changes is activated, you can make edits freely, and all changes will be automatically tracked:

- **Insertions**: Any added text will appear in a different color, underlined or italicized, depending on your settings.

- **Deletions**: Deleted text will be crossed out but still visible, and you'll also see a comment indicating who made the change.
- **Formatting Changes**: Changes in font size, style, or alignment will also be highlighted.

As a reviewer, you can go through these changes and decide what to accept or reject.

Accepting or Rejecting Changes

To review and finalize the changes made by others:

1. **Accepting Changes**: Once you're satisfied with a change, click on the **Accept** button in the **Changes** section of the **Review** tab. You can choose to accept individual changes or all changes at once.
2. **Rejecting Changes**: If you don't want a particular change, click **Reject**. Again, you can reject individual changes or all at once.

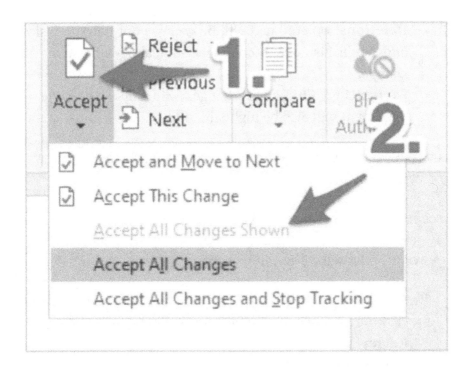

This feature ensures that all edits are transparent, so you can track the document's evolution and make informed decisions about which suggestions to implement.

3. Sharing a Document for Real-Time Collaboration

Real-time collaboration is perhaps one of the most powerful features of Word, especially when using it with Microsoft 365 or OneDrive. By sharing a document online, multiple users can work on the same file simultaneously, no matter where they are in the world.

How to Share a Document for Real-Time Collaboration

1. **Save the Document Online**: To collaborate in real-time, the document must be stored online. You can save it to OneDrive, SharePoint, or Microsoft Teams.

   o Go to **File > Save As**, and select **OneDrive** as the destination to store the file in the cloud.

2. **Share the Document**:

   o Once the document is saved to OneDrive, click the **Share** button located in the upper-right corner of the window.

- You will be prompted to enter the email addresses of the people you want to share the document with, or you can create a link that anyone can use to access the file.
- Set permissions for your collaborators: you can choose whether they can only view the document or if they can edit it as well.

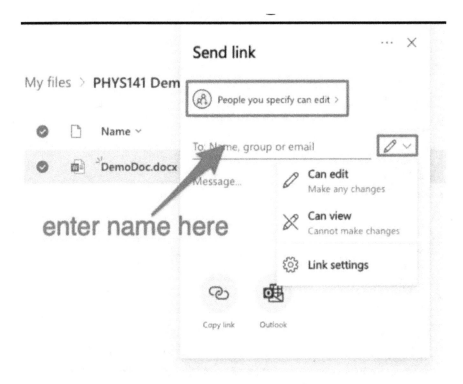

3. **Collaborating in Real-Time**:
   - After sharing the document, collaborators can open it from their own computers, tablets, or smartphones.
   - You'll see their changes in real-time as they happen. Word will highlight the sections where others are

currently editing, and you can even see their cursor moving through the document.

4. **Commenting During Collaboration**: While collaborating in real-time, each user can still add comments and use the **Track Changes** feature. Comments and edits will appear in different colors, making it easy to see who's contributing which changes.

Version History and Reverting Changes

Word also keeps a version history for shared documents. If you ever need to view or restore a previous version:

1. **Access Version History**:
   o In the **File** tab, click **Info** and then select **Version History**.
   o This allows you to view earlier versions of the document and restore them if necessary.

This feature ensures that your document remains intact and that you can go back to previous versions in case any mistakes are made.

4. Best Practices for Collaboration

To ensure a smooth collaboration process, here are a few best practices:

1. **Communicate Regularly**: Whether through comments, emails, or other channels, regular communication is essential when working together. This keeps everyone aligned on the goals and progress.

2. **Set Clear Permissions**: Be clear about who can edit, comment, or only view the document. Having a clear understanding of each team member's role will help prevent confusion.
3. **Use Track Changes Sparingly**: When collaborating on large documents, don't overuse Track Changes. Too many edits can clutter the document, making it hard to focus on the main content. Instead, use comments for suggestions or questions.
4. **Check Document Compatibility**: If your collaborators are using different versions of Word, make sure the document is saved in a format that everyone can open, such as DOCX or PDF.

Conclusion

Microsoft Word offers a robust set of collaboration tools that make working with others on documents straightforward and efficient. By using features like **comments**, **Track Changes**, and **real-time document sharing**, you can ensure that your team stays on the same page, edits are tracked, and feedback is incorporated effectively. These tools not only improve productivity but also foster better communication among collaborators, ultimately resulting in higher-quality documents.

Chapter 15: Mastering Mail Merge in Microsoft Word

Mail Merge is one of the most powerful tools in Microsoft Word, enabling you to create a batch of personalized documents, such as letters, labels, and envelopes, all from a single template. Whether you're sending personalized letters to clients or printing hundreds of address labels for a mailing campaign, Mail Merge can save you time and effort by automating the process.

In this chapter, we'll dive into the step-by-step process of setting up a Mail Merge for letters, creating labels and envelopes, and importing data from Excel or Access databases.

What is Mail Merge?

Mail Merge is a feature that allows you to create a document template (such as a letter, envelope, or label) and merge it with a data source to personalize multiple copies of the document. The data source typically contains information such as names, addresses, and other personalized details that will replace placeholders in your document.

For example, if you're sending out a letter to 100 recipients, you could create one letter with a "Dear [Name]" placeholder. Then, by using a data source (like an Excel spreadsheet with a list of names), Word will automatically insert the appropriate name for each letter.

Setting Up a Mail Merge for Letters

One of the most common uses of Mail Merge is to create personalized letters, such as form letters or holiday greetings. Here's how to set up a Mail Merge for letters in Microsoft Word:

Step 1: Start with a New Document

Begin by opening a new document in Word. If you have an existing letter template, you can use that as your starting point.

Step 2: Open the Mail Merge Wizard

1. Navigate to the **Mailings** tab in the Ribbon.
2. Click on **Start Mail Merge**, then choose **Step-by-Step Mail Merge Wizard**. This opens a sidebar on the right side of your screen to guide you through the entire Mail Merge process.

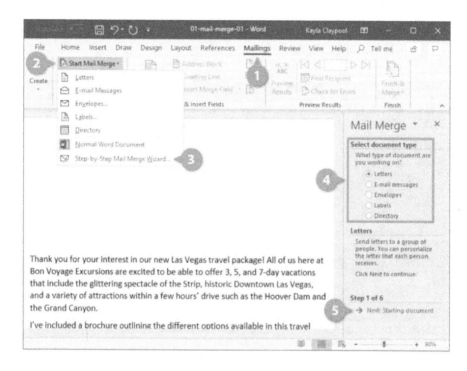

Step 3: Select the Document Type

In the sidebar, you'll be asked to choose the type of document you're creating. For letters, select **Letters** and click **Next**.

Step 4: Select Recipients

To personalize the letters, you'll need to select a data source. You can use a **New List**, **Existing List**, or **Outlook Contacts**:

- **New List**: This allows you to create a new list of names and addresses directly in Word.
- **Existing List**: Use this option to link to a pre-existing list, such as an Excel spreadsheet or Access database, that contains the information.

- **Outlook Contacts**: If your contacts are stored in Outlook, you can link directly to your Outlook contact list.

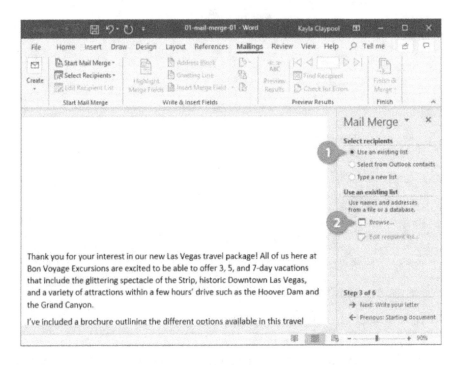

Step 5: Insert Merge Fields

Once you've selected your data source, you'll need to insert merge fields into your letter template where you want personalized information to appear (such as the recipient's name, address, or salutation). In the **Mailings** tab, click **Insert Merge Field**, and you'll see a list of available fields from your data source (e.g., First Name, Last Name, Address). Place the fields where necessary in your document.

Example:

- **Dear <<FirstName>> <<LastName>>,**
- **[Address]**

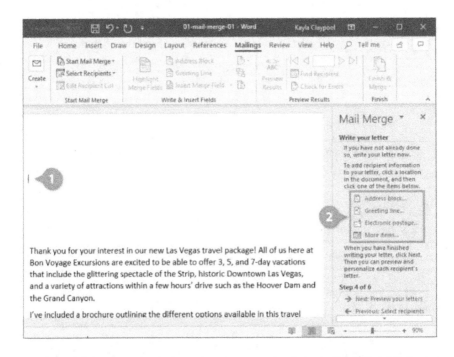

Thank you for your interest in our new Las Vegas travel package! All of us here at Bon Voyage Excursions are excited to be able to offer 3, 5, and 7-day vacations that include the glittering spectacle of the Strip, historic Downtown Las Vegas, and a variety of attractions within a few hours' drive such as the Hoover Dam and the Grand Canyon.

I've included a brochure outlining the different options available in this travel

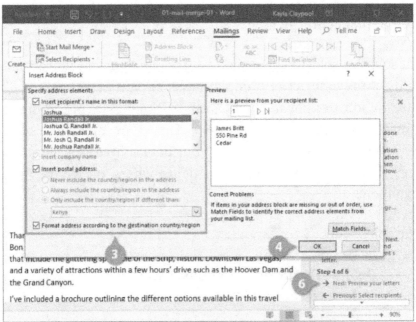

Click on **Preview Results** to check how the merged fields will look with actual data from your list.

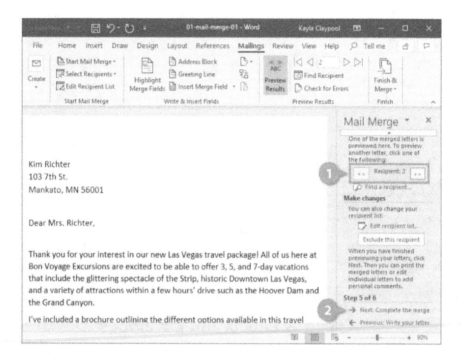

Step 6: Complete the Merge

Once you're satisfied with the setup, click **Finish & Merge** in the Mail Merge pane. You can then:

- **Print Documents**: Directly print the letters.
- **Create a New Document**: This option will generate a new Word document containing all of the personalized letters, which you can review or save.

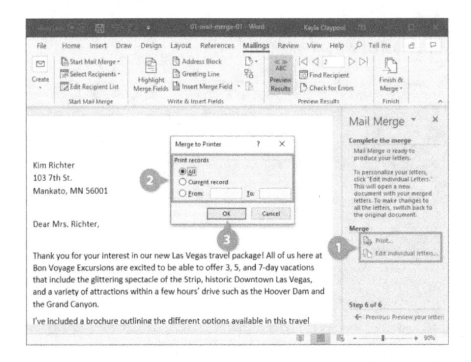

Creating Labels and Envelopes

Mail Merge can also be used to create address labels and envelopes for bulk mailings. The process is similar to setting up a letter merge, but instead of creating a letter, you're generating a label or envelope template.

Creating Address Labels

1. **Open a New Document** and go to the **Mailings** tab.
2. Click on **Start Mail Merge** and select **Labels**.

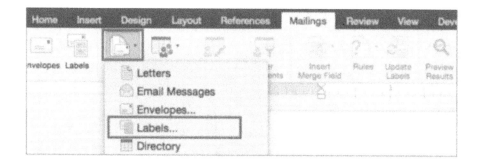

3. In the **Label Options** dialog box, choose the type of label you want to use (such as Avery, or custom sizes).

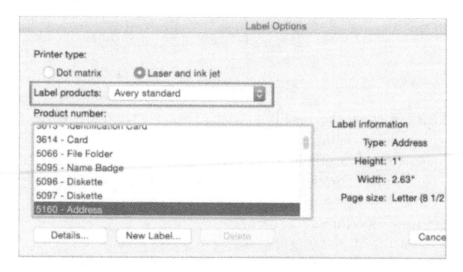

4. Select your data source and insert the merge fields, just as you did for the letter. Typically, you'll insert the recipient's **Name**, **Address**, and **City, State, Zip** into the label format.

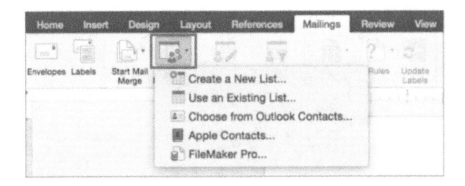

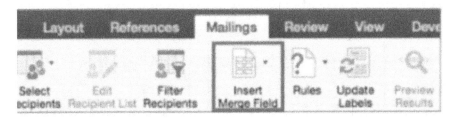

5. Preview the results to make sure everything is correctly placed on the labels.
6. Once everything looks good, click **Finish & Merge**, then either print the labels or create a new document to save.

Creating Envelopes

If you're sending physical letters, Mail Merge can also help you create personalized envelopes:

1. **Open a New Document** and go to the **Mailings** tab.
2. Click on **Start Mail Merge** and select **Envelopes**.
3. Choose your envelope size (e.g., #10, DL) in the **Envelope Options**.

4. Insert the recipient's address using merge fields from your data source (e.g., **FirstName, LastName, Address**, etc.) into the envelope template.
5. As with labels, preview the result to ensure the address fields are positioned correctly.
6. Click **Finish & Merge** to either print the envelopes directly or generate a new document.

Importing Data from Excel or Access

To make the most of Mail Merge, you often need a data source that contains the details for personalization—like names, addresses, phone numbers, and other relevant information. Microsoft Word can easily import data from both **Excel** and **Access** databases. Here's how:

Importing Data from Excel

1. **Prepare Your Excel Spreadsheet**: Organize your data with clear column headers (e.g., First Name, Last Name, Address, City, etc.).
2. **Select Your Data Source**:
   o In Word, go to the **Mailings** tab and click **Select Recipients**.
   o Choose **Use an Existing List** and navigate to the Excel file where your data is stored.
3. **Link the Data**: Once the file is selected, a dialog box will pop up, showing you a preview of your data. Select the worksheet that contains your contact information and ensure all necessary fields are included.

Importing Data from Access

If you're using Microsoft Access to store your contact information, the process is very similar:

1. **Prepare Your Database**: Ensure that your contact information is stored in an Access table with appropriate fields.
2. **Select the Data Source**:
   o In Word, click **Select Recipients** and choose **Use an Existing List**.
   o Locate your Access database file and select the relevant table or query that contains your data.
3. **Link the Data**: Once you choose the table or query, Word will pull in the information for Mail Merge, and you can begin inserting merge fields into your document as needed.

Troubleshooting Common Mail Merge Issues

While Mail Merge is generally straightforward, there are a few common issues you might run into:

- **Missing or Incorrect Data**: If some fields aren't merging properly, ensure that your data source is formatted correctly. Make sure there are no blank rows or columns, and that every field has the correct information.
- **Field Formatting Issues**: Sometimes, merged fields may appear with strange formatting (such as date fields displaying incorrectly). You can fix this by right-clicking on the field and selecting **Edit Field** or adjusting the field code.

- **Data Source Not Updating**: If you update your Excel or Access data after linking it to Word, you may need to refresh the connection. In Word, go to **Mailings > Edit Recipient List** and click **Refresh** to reload the data.

Conclusion

Mail Merge is a fantastic tool that can help you create personalized documents in bulk, saving you significant time and effort. Whether you're creating letters, labels, or envelopes, the process is quick and easy with the Mail Merge wizard in Microsoft Word. By importing data from Excel or Access, you can ensure that each document is tailored to the recipient, increasing the professional appeal of your communications. With a little practice, Mail Merge will become an indispensable part of your document workflow.

Chapter 16: Printing and Exporting Documents

O nce your document is perfectly polished and ready to be shared or printed, Microsoft Word provides a variety of tools to help you finalize and export your work in the way that best suits your needs. This chapter will guide you through the essential steps for printing, adjusting settings, and exporting your document to various formats. You'll learn how to preview your document before printing, select the correct paper size, and explore options for exporting to formats such as PDF.

1. Print Preview and Print Settings

Before you hit the **Print** button, it's always a good idea to preview your document. This ensures everything looks exactly the way you want it, from text alignment to image positioning. Word's **Print Preview** feature allows you to examine your document and adjust any settings to avoid any surprises once you print. Here's how you can access the print preview and tweak your print settings:

Accessing Print Preview:

1. Click on the **File** tab in the Ribbon to open the **Backstage View**.

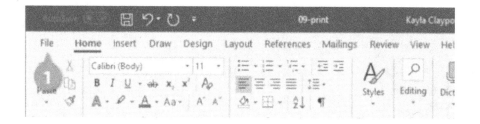

2. From the menu, select **Print** (you can also press **Ctrl + P** to quickly open this section).
3. This will display the **Print Preview** of your document on the right side of the screen, along with the **Print Settings** on the left.

Adjusting Print Settings: In the **Print Settings** area, you will see several important options you can adjust before printing:

- **Printer Selection**: Choose which printer you'd like to use. If you're connected to multiple printers, you can select from the available options.
- **Pages**: Select which pages to print, such as all pages, a range of pages (e.g., pages 1-5), or specific pages (e.g., pages 1, 3, and 5).
- **Copies**: Adjust the number of copies to print. If you need multiple copies, simply increase the number.
- **Print on Both Sides**: If your printer supports duplex printing, you can choose to print on both sides of the paper to save space and paper.

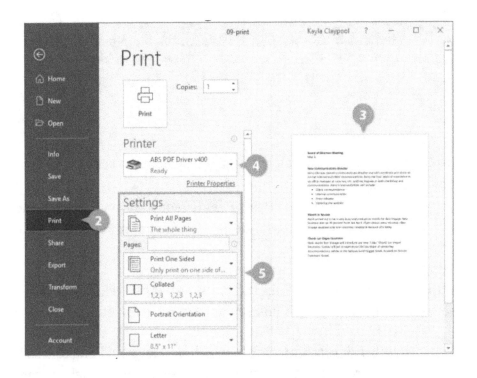

The **Print Preview** shows how your document will appear on the page, including margins, headers/footers, and any images. This is the time to make sure everything is positioned correctly and that no part of your text or graphics is cut off.

2. Selecting Paper Size and Layout

Choosing the right paper size and layout is essential to ensure your document looks professional when printed. Word allows you to modify the paper size, orientation, and layout before printing, depending on your needs.

Adjusting Paper Size: The **paper size** determines how your content fits on the printed page. Common paper sizes include

Letter (8.5 x 11 inches), **A4** (8.27 x 11.69 inches), and **Legal** (8.5 x 14 inches). To change the paper size:

1. Go to the **Layout** tab in the Ribbon.
2. Click on the **Size** button.
3. From the drop-down menu, choose the paper size that suits your document. If you need a custom size, select **More Paper Sizes** at the bottom, where you can enter specific measurements.

Changing Page Orientation: You can switch between **Portrait** (vertical) and **Landscape** (horizontal) orientation, depending on how you want your content to appear. To change the orientation:

1. In the **Layout** tab, click on the **Orientation** button.
2. Choose between **Portrait** and **Landscape**.
   - **Portrait** is commonly used for standard text documents.
   - **Landscape** is ideal for wide content, like spreadsheets, charts, or wide tables.

Setting Margins: The margin settings define the space between the text and the edges of the page. Word offers several preset margin options (e.g., Normal, Narrow, Wide), but you can also set custom margins.

1. Go to the **Layout** tab.
2. Click on **Margins** and select a preset or choose **Custom Margins** to input your desired margin sizes.

Header/Footer Placement: Headers and footers appear at the top and bottom of your document, respectively. They're useful for displaying page numbers, titles, and other consistent information throughout the document.

1. Navigate to the **Insert** tab.
2. Select **Header** or **Footer**.
3. Choose from various styles or create a custom header/footer for your document.

3. Exporting to PDF and Other Formats

Once your document is ready to be shared or archived, Word provides a range of export options. **PDF** (Portable Document Format) is the most commonly used format for sharing documents because it preserves the layout and formatting across different devices. Word also supports exporting documents to other formats, such as **XPS** or **HTML**. Here's how to export your document:

Exporting to PDF:

1. Click on the **File** tab.
2. Select **Save As**.
3. Choose where you want to save your document (e.g., computer, OneDrive).
4. In the **Save As Type** dropdown menu, select **PDF**.
5. Click **Save**.
   - Word offers an option to **Optimize for Standard** or **Minimum size**. The **Standard** option is best for printing, while the **Minimum size** option is ideal for sharing documents via email or the web, as it reduces file size.

Exporting to XPS: XPS (XML Paper Specification) is similar to PDF but is primarily used for sharing with other Windows users. To save your document as an XPS file:

1. Follow the same steps as exporting to PDF, but choose **XPS Document** as the file type.
2. Click **Save** to complete the export.

Saving as an Image: In some cases, you may want to save your document as an image (such as **JPEG** or **PNG**) for use in presentations or for sharing on social media.

1. Select the portion of the document you want to save as an image.
2. Take a screenshot or use a third-party tool to capture the image.
3. Save it in your desired format.

Exporting to HTML: If you're working on content intended for a website or online platform, exporting your document to HTML may be necessary. To do so:

1. Go to **File > Save As**.
2. In the **Save as type** dropdown menu, choose **Web Page (.htm; .html)**.
3. Click **Save** to export your document.

4. Printing to PDF

For those who need to print a document without actually using a printer, Word offers a virtual printer option called **Microsoft Print**

to PDF. This lets you "print" your document directly into a PDF file instead of paper.

To print to PDF:

1. Click **File > Print**.
2. In the **Printer** dropdown, choose **Microsoft Print to PDF**.
3. Adjust any other settings (like number of copies or page range).
4. Click **Print** and choose a location to save the PDF file.

This option is especially useful for digital records, email sharing, or archiving important documents.

5. Sending to an Email

If you want to email your document directly from Word without saving it to your computer first, you can do so by using the **Email** option:

1. Click **File > Share > Email**.
2. Choose between **Send as Attachment** or **Send as PDF**.
3. Word will automatically open your default email client with the document attached, ready for you to address and send.

This feature streamlines the process when you need to send a document immediately, without having to manually open your email client.

Conclusion

Whether you're preparing a document for printing, sharing, or archiving, Word offers numerous options for ensuring your document is formatted exactly the way you want it. By using the **Print Preview** feature, adjusting paper size and layout, and exporting to PDF or other formats, you can ensure your work looks professional, no matter how it's delivered. Understanding how to manage print settings and export documents will save you time and effort, ensuring you're always ready to present your work in the best possible format.

Chapter 17: Document Security

In today's digital world, document security is paramount. Whether you're working on a sensitive report, a personal project, or collaborating with colleagues, it's essential to ensure that your document remains secure and that unauthorized access or alterations are prevented. Microsoft Word provides several tools to help safeguard your work, whether through password protection, restricting editing capabilities, or inspecting your document for potentially sensitive information. In this chapter, we will explore these key security features in detail to help you manage and protect your documents.

1. Protecting Your Document with Passwords

One of the most effective ways to secure a document is by setting a password. By doing so, you restrict access to only those who have the password, ensuring that unauthorized users cannot open or edit your document. Let's walk through how to set a password for your Word document:

Setting a Password for Opening the Document

1. **Open your document** in Microsoft Word.

2. Click on the **File** tab in the Ribbon to access the **Backstage View**.
3. From the list of options on the left, click **Info**. This section provides a variety of document settings, including the option to protect your document.
4. In the **Protect Document** section, click on **Encrypt with Password**.

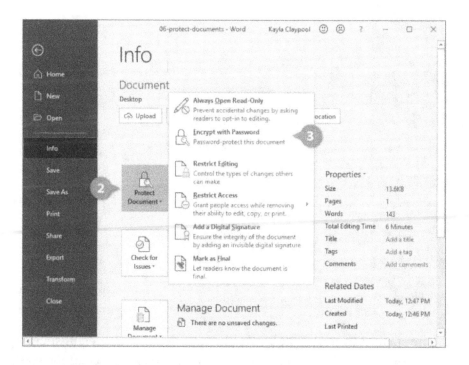

5. A dialog box will appear, prompting you to enter a password. Choose a strong password that includes a combination of uppercase and lowercase letters, numbers, and special characters. Ensure the password is memorable or store it securely, as losing the password will prevent you from accessing the document.

6. After entering the password, click **OK**. You will be asked to re-enter the password to confirm it.

7. Once confirmed, your document is now password-protected, and anyone who tries to open it will be prompted to enter the password.

It's important to note that while passwords are a powerful security measure, they should be used carefully. Choosing a weak or easily guessed password could compromise your document's security, so always use a strong password. If you need to share your document with someone, make sure you securely convey the password.

Setting a Password to Restrict Editing

In some cases, you might want to allow someone to view your document but prevent them from making any changes to it. Microsoft Word lets you set up restrictions to allow only certain parts of the document to be edited, or to prevent editing entirely. Here's how:

1. Open your document and go to the **File** tab.

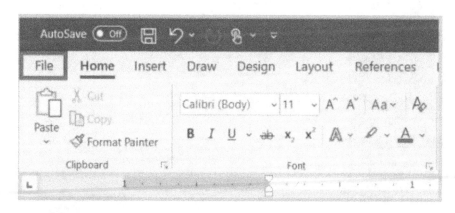

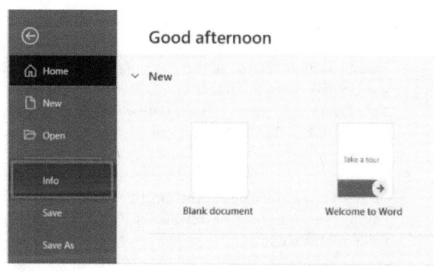

2. In the **Info** section, select **Protect Document**, then click on **Restrict Editing**.

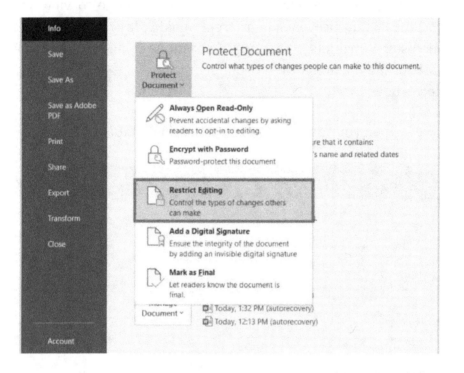

3. In the **Restrict Editing** pane on the right, you'll find several options for restricting editing. You can limit editing to specific sections, allow only formatting changes, or prevent any changes to the document.
4. To prevent any editing, select **Allow only this type of editing in the document** and choose **No changes (Read only)**.
5. If you wish to apply a password for restricting editing, click on **Yes, Start Enforcing Protection**, then set a password for editing. This ensures that anyone trying to make changes will need the password.

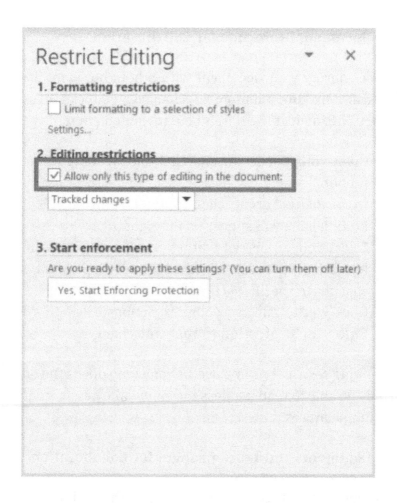

2. Restricting Editing for Shared Files

When collaborating with others, you may want to allow them to read your document but restrict their ability to make edits. Microsoft Word offers several features to control how others can interact with your document while maintaining the integrity of its content.

Using Document Protection for Collaboration

If you're sharing your document with others but want to prevent them from making unintended changes, you can use Word's **Restrict Editing** feature. Here's how to implement it:

1. Open your document and click on the **Review** tab in the Ribbon.
2. In the **Protect** group, click on **Restrict Editing**. The Restrict Editing pane will appear on the right.
3. Select your preferred editing restrictions. You can restrict formatting, prevent any changes to the content, or limit changes to specific sections.
4. Once you've selected your restrictions, click on **Yes, Start Enforcing Protection** to apply the changes.

With editing restrictions in place, anyone who opens the document will only be able to read it unless they know the password to unlock the editing features.

Using Comments and Track Changes for Collaboration

When working with collaborators, rather than allowing them to directly edit the document, you may want to enable **Track Changes** and **Comments**. This way, you can keep track of all suggestions, edits, and additions made by others, which can then be reviewed and accepted or rejected.

1. Go to the **Review** tab in the Ribbon.
2. Click on **Track Changes** to enable the feature. This will highlight any text added or deleted by other users.

3. Use the **New Comment** option to leave comments for others to review.
4. When you're done, you can choose to **Accept** or **Reject** any changes made to the document.

This ensures that your document remains intact and that any changes are made in a controlled, transparent way.

3. Inspecting Documents for Sensitive Information

Before sharing or distributing a document, it's important to check for any hidden or sensitive information that might not be visible at first glance. Microsoft Word provides an invaluable tool called the **Document Inspector**, which helps detect hidden metadata, comments, tracked changes, or even personal information that might have been inadvertently included in your document. Here's how to use it:

Using the Document Inspector

1. Open the document you want to inspect.
2. Click on the **File** tab to enter the **Backstage View**.
3. In the **Info** section, click on **Check for Issues** and select **Inspect Document**.

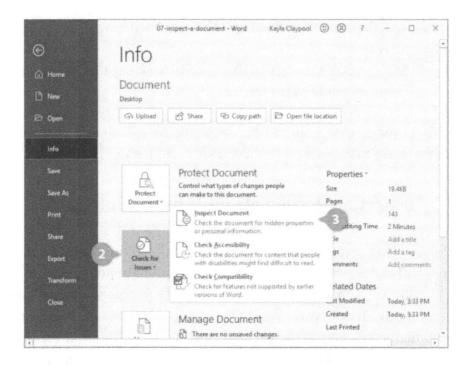

4. The Document Inspector dialog box will appear. You can choose to check for different types of content, including:
   o **Comments and annotations**
   o **Document properties and personal information**
   o **Hidden text and tracked changes**
   o **Invisible content like annotations or headers**
5. After selecting the types of content you want to search for, click **Inspect**.

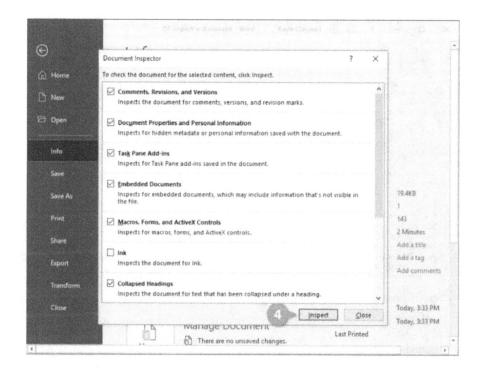

6. The Document Inspector will show a summary of all the content it found. You can then choose to **Remove All** or simply view the content to decide whether to delete it.

This tool is especially useful when you are preparing documents for sharing with external parties or colleagues and want to ensure that confidential data such as tracked changes, personal information, or hidden comments aren't inadvertently exposed.

Additional Security Tips

While the password protection, editing restrictions, and document inspection features in Microsoft Word provide a strong foundation for securing your documents, it's always a good idea to follow additional best practices for document security:

1. **Store Documents Securely**: Use cloud services like OneDrive or SharePoint for secure document storage,

ensuring your documents are protected with additional layers of encryption.

2. **Back Up Important Documents**: Regularly back up your files to ensure you don't lose important work in case of technical issues or data corruption.
3. **Use Two-Factor Authentication (2FA)**: Enable two-factor authentication for your cloud storage and email accounts to provide an extra layer of security when accessing your documents online.
4. **Review Permissions**: If you're collaborating on a document stored in the cloud, regularly check and update sharing permissions to make sure only the intended users have access.

By implementing these measures and regularly reviewing the security of your documents, you can be confident that your work is protected from unauthorized access, alterations, and other security threats.

In conclusion, Microsoft Word offers robust security features that enable you to protect, manage, and share your documents with confidence. By setting strong passwords, restricting editing capabilities, and inspecting documents for sensitive content, you can ensure your work remains safe and secure, whether you're working on a personal project or collaborating with others.

Chapter 18: Common Problems and Solutions

E ven with the powerful features Microsoft Word offers, it's not uncommon to encounter a few hiccups when working on a document. Fortunately, most issues are easily fixable with just a few steps. This chapter will guide you through some of the most frequent problems Word users face, along with effective solutions to help you resolve them. From formatting headaches to alignment struggles and the occasional file recovery, you'll find practical solutions here.

1. Resolving Formatting Issues

Formatting issues can often be the most frustrating to deal with, especially when your document looks great one moment and chaotic the next. These issues can arise from inconsistent fonts, line spacing, margins, and paragraph styles. Fortunately, Microsoft Word provides several tools that can help you regain control of your document's appearance.

Inconsistent Fonts or Text Styles

One of the most common formatting issues users face is inconsistent fonts or text styles. This can happen when you copy and paste content from another document or website, which might bring with it hidden formatting codes.

Solution:

- **Clear Formatting**: To remove any unwanted formatting, highlight the text in question, go to the **Home** tab, and click **Clear All Formatting** in the **Font** section. This will strip the text of any external styles.
- **Use Styles**: To ensure consistency throughout your document, use **Styles** (found in the **Home** tab). Styles allow you to apply predefined formatting to headings, subheadings, and body text, making your document uniform and easily editable.

Inconsistent Line Spacing

Sometimes, line spacing can appear inconsistent throughout your document, with some paragraphs looking cramped and others too spread out.

Solution:

- **Adjust Line Spacing**: Highlight the affected paragraphs, right-click, and select **Paragraph**. In the dialog box that appears, ensure that the line spacing is set to your desired option (e.g., **Single**, **1.5 lines**, or **Double**).
- **Remove Extra Paragraph Spacing**: If extra space appears between paragraphs, make sure the "Before" and "After" settings in the Paragraph dialog box are set to **0 pt**. This will eliminate unnecessary gaps between paragraphs.

Misaligned Text

Misaligned text can disrupt the flow of your document, whether it's content that seems out of place, uneven margins, or text that won't align as expected.

Solution:

- **Check Alignment Settings**: Select the text that is misaligned, and in the **Home** tab, use the alignment options (**Left**, **Center**, **Right**, or **Justify**) to fix the positioning of your text. You can also use keyboard shortcuts: **Ctrl + L** (Left), **Ctrl + E** (Center), **Ctrl + R** (Right), and **Ctrl + J** (Justify).
- **Use the Ruler**: If the text is still misaligned despite using the alignment tools, turn on the ruler by clicking **View** and checking **Ruler**. Use the ruler to adjust the indentations for your paragraphs or the whole document.

Page and Section Break Issues

Unexpected page or section breaks can also create formatting problems, especially if your content moves to the next page when it shouldn't.

Solution:

- **Show Formatting Marks**: To see where breaks are located, go to the **Home** tab and click ¶ to show formatting marks. Look for section breaks or page breaks that may be causing unwanted gaps or layout shifts.

- **Remove Breaks**: If you find any unwanted page or section breaks, simply click on the break symbol and press the **Delete** key to remove it.

2. Fixing Alignment and Spacing Problems

Even when formatting seems fine, alignment and spacing issues can still crop up. These problems typically occur when working with tables, images, or complex layouts, and they can significantly affect the readability of your document.

Inconsistent Margins

Sometimes the margins in your document might appear uneven, with text spilling over the edges or sections of the page looking misaligned.

Solution:

- **Adjust Margins**: Go to the **Layout** tab, and in the **Page Setup** group, click **Margins**. Choose a preset margin or select **Custom Margins** to set your desired top, bottom, left, and right margins.
- **Check for Section Breaks**: Different sections of your document can have different margin settings. Ensure that there are no section breaks that are affecting margin settings in specific parts of your document.

Text Box and Image Alignment Problems

Placing text boxes or images in your document might cause alignment issues, especially if text is flowing around them incorrectly or the objects appear off-center.

Solution:

- **Use Text Wrapping**: Select the image or text box, go to the **Picture Format** or **Text Box Tools** tab, and choose a text wrapping option like **Square**, **Tight**, or **Behind Text**. This will adjust the text flow around the object and prevent overlap.
- **Align Objects Using the Grid**: If you're having trouble aligning images or objects manually, you can use the **Align** options in the **Arrange** group under the **Picture Format** tab. Choose options like **Align Left**, **Align Center**, or **Align Right** to align objects relative to the page or margins.

Paragraph Spacing Problems

Paragraph spacing problems are often a result of inconsistent settings for **Before** and **After** spacing.

Solution:

- **Adjust Paragraph Spacing**: Right-click on the paragraph and select **Paragraph**. Under the **Spacing** section, ensure that both the **Before** and **After** spacing are set to the same value (or **0 pt** if no extra spacing is desired).
- **Use Styles for Consistent Spacing**: For documents that require multiple types of spacing (e.g., for headings,

subheadings, and body text), create and apply custom paragraph styles to ensure consistent spacing throughout the document.

3. Recovering Lost or Corrupted Files

It's every writer's worst nightmare—losing work due to a crash or file corruption. Fortunately, Word offers several built-in recovery tools to help you retrieve lost or corrupted files.

AutoRecover

Microsoft Word has an **AutoRecover** feature that automatically saves versions of your document at regular intervals. If Word crashes or closes unexpectedly, you can usually recover the most recent version of your file.

Solution:

- **Open AutoRecovered Files**: After reopening Word, look for the **Document Recovery** pane on the left side of the screen. If your document is listed there, click it to open the most recent version.
- **Manually Check for AutoRecovered Files**: If you don't see the document in the Document Recovery pane, go to **File > Info > Manage Document > Recover Unsaved Documents**. This will show a list of unsaved documents from your most recent sessions.

Recovering Corrupted Files

Corrupted files can prevent you from opening or editing your document. This often occurs if the file was improperly closed, or if there's an issue with the storage device.

Solution:

- **Open in Safe Mode**: If Word won't open a file, try opening it in **Safe Mode**. Hold **Ctrl** while opening Word to prevent add-ins from loading. Once Word opens, attempt to open the corrupted document.
- **Recover Text from Any File**: If a document is severely corrupted, you can try opening it as a **Plain Text** file. Go to **File > Open**, and under **Files of Type**, choose **Recover Text from Any File**. This will extract plain text from the document, though it may lose formatting.

Backing Up Documents Regularly

Prevent data loss by regularly saving backup copies of your documents. You can configure Word to save backup versions every time you save a file.

Solution:

- **Set Up Backup Files**: To enable Word to automatically create backup copies of your document, go to **File > Options > Advanced**. Scroll down to the **Save** section and check **Always create backup copy**.

Chapter 19: Time-Saving Tips

As you dive deeper into Microsoft Word, you'll discover various features and techniques designed to streamline your work and increase productivity. In this chapter, we'll explore some of the most effective time-saving tips that will help you work faster and more efficiently. These include using **keyboard shortcuts**, customizing the **Quick Access Toolbar**, and creating **macros** for automating repetitive tasks.

1. Using Keyboard Shortcuts

Keyboard shortcuts are one of the easiest and quickest ways to save time while working in Microsoft Word. Instead of clicking through menus and tabs, you can perform most actions with a simple combination of keys. By learning these shortcuts, you can keep your hands on the keyboard and avoid constantly switching between the mouse and keyboard.

Let's take a look at some of the most commonly used keyboard shortcuts in Word:

Basic Text Editing Shortcuts:

- **Ctrl + C**: Copy the selected text or object.
- **Ctrl + X**: Cut the selected text or object.

- **Ctrl + V**: Paste the copied or cut text or object.
- **Ctrl + Z**: Undo the last action.
- **Ctrl + Y**: Redo the last undone action.
- **Ctrl + A**: Select all text or content in the document.
- **Ctrl + B**: Toggle bold formatting.
- **Ctrl + I**: Toggle italics formatting.
- **Ctrl + U**: Toggle underline formatting.
- **Ctrl + S**: Save the document.

Navigating the Document:

- **Ctrl + Home**: Move to the beginning of the document.
- **Ctrl + End**: Move to the end of the document.
- **Ctrl + Left Arrow**: Move one word to the left.
- **Ctrl + Right Arrow**: Move one word to the right.
- **Ctrl + Up Arrow**: Move one paragraph up.
- **Ctrl + Down Arrow**: Move one paragraph down.

Formatting and Other Useful Shortcuts:

- **Ctrl + E**: Center-align the text.
- **Ctrl + L**: Left-align the text.
- **Ctrl + R**: Right-align the text.
- **Ctrl + J**: Justify the text (spread it evenly across the page).
- **Ctrl + T**: Create a hanging indent.
- **Ctrl + M**: Increase the left indent by one level.
- **Ctrl + Shift + N**: Apply the Normal style.
- **Ctrl + Shift + L**: Apply the List style.

Search and Replace:

- **Ctrl + F**: Open the Find and Replace dialog to search for text in the document.
- **Ctrl + H**: Open the Find and Replace dialog with the option to replace text.

These shortcuts are just the tip of the iceberg. As you grow more comfortable with them, you'll find that they can drastically reduce the amount of time you spend navigating through the interface and performing basic tasks.

2. Customizing the Quick Access Toolbar

The **Quick Access Toolbar (QAT)** is a powerful feature in Microsoft Word that gives you immediate access to the tools you use most frequently. By default, the QAT is located at the top of the screen, just above the Ribbon. It includes commands such as **Save**, **Undo**, and **Redo**. However, Word allows you to customize this toolbar so that it fits your unique needs and preferences.

Here's how you can customize the QAT:

Adding Commands to the Quick Access Toolbar:

1. **Open Word** and locate the Quick Access Toolbar at the top-left corner of the window.
2. Click on the small drop-down arrow at the end of the toolbar.
3. From the list of available commands, you can either select one of the common commands or choose **More Commands** to access a full list of options.

4. In the **Word Options** dialog that appears, select the command you want to add (such as **Print Preview**, **Copy**, or **Paste**), then click **Add**.
5. Once added, the command will appear in the QAT. You can also rearrange the order by selecting the command and using the **Up** or **Down** buttons.

Removing Commands from the Quick Access Toolbar:

To remove a command from the QAT, follow these steps:

1. Right-click on the command you want to remove in the Quick Access Toolbar.
2. Select **Remove from Quick Access Toolbar** from the context menu.

Customizing the Position of the QAT:

By default, the QAT is located above the Ribbon, but you can choose to move it below the Ribbon if you prefer:

1. Right-click on the Quick Access Toolbar.
2. Select **Show Below the Ribbon** to move the QAT beneath the Ribbon for easier access.

Adding Your Most Used Tools:

Consider adding the following commands to your QAT for faster access:

- **Bold, Italic, Underline**: If you frequently apply text formatting.

- **Page Break**: If you often need to insert page breaks.
- **Insert Table**: If you work with tables regularly.
- **Save As**: If you need to frequently save your work under different file names or formats.

Customizing your Quick Access Toolbar means you can bypass the Ribbon and access your favorite tools immediately, cutting down on time spent searching for specific commands.

3. Creating Macros for Repetitive Tasks

If you find yourself performing the same tasks over and over again, creating **macros** in Microsoft Word can save you a lot of time. A macro is a series of actions or commands that you can record and then replay with a single click or keyboard shortcut. Macros are especially useful for tasks that involve multiple steps, such as formatting text, inserting tables, or even generating reports.

Recording a Macro:

1. Go to the **View** tab on the Ribbon.
2. In the **Macros** group, click **Record Macro**.
3. In the **Record Macro** dialog box, give your macro a name and choose whether you want to assign a **button** or a **keyboard shortcut** for quick access.
4. You can choose to store the macro in either the current document or in the **Normal.dotm** template so that it's available across all documents.
5. After naming your macro and assigning a shortcut (if desired), click **OK**.

6. Now, Word will start recording all the actions you perform. Complete the series of actions that you want the macro to perform (such as formatting a section of text, inserting a table, etc.).
7. Once you've completed your actions, go back to the **View** tab and click **Stop Recording**.

Running a Macro:

To run the macro you just recorded:

1. Go to the **View** tab, click **Macros**, and choose **View Macros**.
2. In the list, select your macro and click **Run**.

Alternatively, if you assigned a keyboard shortcut to the macro, simply press that shortcut, and the macro will execute all the recorded actions.

Editing a Macro:

If you need to make changes to a macro, you can do so through the **Visual Basic for Applications (VBA)** editor:

1. Go to the **View** tab, click **Macros**, and choose **View Macros**.
2. Select the macro you want to edit and click **Edit**.
3. This will open the VBA editor, where you can view the code and make modifications.

Creating macros is an excellent way to automate common tasks, and once you've set up a macro, you'll save a tremendous amount of time on repetitive operations.

Common Uses for Macros in Word:

- **Standardizing formatting**: Apply a specific style to text, headings, or paragraphs.
- **Inserting predefined text**: Automatically insert boilerplate content such as legal disclaimers, company addresses, or email signatures.
- **Document cleanup**: Perform multiple clean-up tasks such as removing extra spaces, correcting formatting issues, and more.

Additional Time-Saving Tips

While keyboard shortcuts, customizing the Quick Access Toolbar, and macros are some of the most powerful time-saving tools, here are a few more tips that can help speed up your workflow:

1. Use Templates for Repetitive Documents

Instead of starting from scratch every time you create a document, consider using **templates**. Templates provide predefined layouts, styles, and content, so all you need to do is fill in the blanks. You can find templates for resumes, newsletters, reports, and even invitations within Word. If you create documents that follow a specific format, create your own templates and save them for future use.

2. Use Styles for Consistent Formatting

Instead of manually adjusting font sizes, line spacing, and other formatting settings every time, use **styles**. Word offers a variety of built-in styles for headings, body text, and other elements. You can even create and customize your own styles to maintain consistency throughout your document.

3. Use the Research and Thesaurus Tools

If you're writing a document that requires research, Word's built-in **Research** and **Thesaurus** tools can save you a great deal of time. Access these tools via the **Review** tab and use them to quickly find synonyms, definitions, or information from online resources.

Chapter 20: Practice Exercises

Practice makes perfect—and this holds especially true when learning new software like Microsoft Word. The more you practice, the more proficient you'll become with the various features and functions. This chapter is designed to provide a variety of hands-on exercises to reinforce the concepts you've learned in the previous chapters. By completing these beginner-level tasks, you will gain confidence in your Word skills and become more comfortable navigating the software.

Through these exercises, you'll work on real-world projects such as creating resumes, writing newsletters, and designing professional documents. These projects will give you a solid understanding of the features Word offers, and how to apply them to create polished and presentable documents.

1. Beginner-Level Tasks to Reinforce Learning

These tasks are designed to help you practice the core skills you've learned so far in Microsoft Word. From typing basic text to formatting paragraphs and adjusting page layouts, these exercises will challenge you to apply the knowledge in real-life scenarios.

Exercise 1: Typing a Simple Letter

Objective: Practice basic typing, text formatting, and layout skills.

Instructions:

1. **Open Microsoft Word** and create a new blank document.
2. **Type the following letter**:

   [Your Name] [Your Address]
   [City, State, ZIP]
   [Phone Number]
   [Email Address]
   [Date]

   Dear [Recipient's Name],

   I hope this letter finds you well. I wanted to take the time to introduce myself and share some important information with you regarding our upcoming project. I look forward to discussing the details and collaborating to ensure its success.

   Please feel free to reach out to me if you have any questions or need additional information. I am excited to get started!

   Thank you for your time, and I look forward to your response.

   Best regards,
   [Your Name]

3. **Apply formatting** to your text:
   - Make your name bold.
   - Italicize the date.
   - Adjust the alignment of the letter to "Justify."
   - Use a different font and font size for the heading.

Goal: This exercise will help you practice basic text entry, formatting, and page layout settings.

Exercise 2: Creating a Bulleted List

Objective: Learn how to create lists, both bulleted and numbered, and how to organize content.

Instructions:

1. **Open a new blank document**.
2. **Type the following information** as a bulleted list:
   - Best practices for creating effective Word documents
   - Formatting headings and subheadings
   - Adding and resizing images
   - Using headers and footers
   - Creating and saving templates
   - Protecting documents with passwords
3. **Format the list**:
   - Add a numbered list to the items.
   - Change the bullet style to a checkmark.
   - Adjust the indentation and alignment of the list.

Goal: This task helps you practice using the bulleting and numbering features, as well as adjusting list formatting options.

Exercise 3: Inserting a Table

Objective: Learn how to create, format, and manage tables in Word.

Instructions:

1. **Create a new document** and insert a table with 3 columns and 4 rows.
2. **Label the columns**: "Item," "Quantity," and "Price."
3. **Fill in the table with sample data**:

Item	Quantity	Price
Apples	10	$5.00
Bananas	6	$2.00
Oranges	8	$4.00

1. **Format the table**:
   o   Adjust the width of the columns.
   o   Apply a table style for a more professional look.
   o   Change the font size for the headers.
   o   Center the text in each cell.
   o   Use the "Shading" option to highlight the header row.

Goal: By completing this exercise, you'll become more familiar with creating and formatting tables, which is an essential skill for organizing and presenting information.

Exercise 4: Inserting an Image and Wrapping Text

Objective: Gain experience with inserting and positioning images, and using text wrapping for a better layout.

Instructions:

1. **Create a new document** and type the following paragraph:

   "Microsoft Word is an incredibly versatile tool. With Word, you can create documents ranging from simple letters to complex reports, and everything in between. Inserting images can help make your documents more engaging and visually appealing. It's important to format these images correctly so they don't disrupt the flow of your content."

2. **Insert an image** of your choice by going to the **Insert** tab and selecting **Pictures**.
3. **Apply text wrapping**:
   o Click on the image, then go to the **Layout Options** icon.
   o Choose the **Square** text wrapping style.
   o Resize and position the image next to the text.
4. **Adjust the layout**:
   o Change the size of the image to fit better with the text.
   o Move the image so it aligns well with the paragraph.

Goal: This exercise will help you understand how to insert images, resize them, and apply text wrapping for better document layout.

2. Sample Projects for Practical Experience

In this section, you'll work on more detailed sample projects that simulate real-world tasks. These projects will allow you to use all the features you've learned so far and apply them to real documents.

Project 1: Creating a Resume

Objective: Learn how to design a professional resume using templates, tables, and formatting.

Instructions:

1. **Open Microsoft Word** and go to **File > New**. Select a resume template that suits your style.
2. **Fill in your personal information**:
   - Contact details (name, address, phone number, email).
   - Objective statement.
   - Education background.
   - Work experience.
   - Skills and certifications.
3. **Format your text**:
   - Make your name bold and increase its font size.
   - Adjust the layout for each section so that the information is clear and easy to read.
   - Use bullet points for listing your skills and responsibilities.
4. **Insert a professional photo**:
   - If desired, you can insert a picture of yourself (optional) by going to the **Insert** tab and selecting **Pictures**.
5. **Save and print the resume** when you're finished.

Goal: This project helps you create a polished resume, which you can later customize and use when applying for jobs.

Project 2: Writing a Newsletter

Objective: Practice using advanced Word features to design a newsletter.

Instructions:

1. **Open a blank document** and create a heading for your newsletter. Use a larger, bold font for the title and make it centered.
2. **Insert a table of contents** to organize the different sections of your newsletter.
3. **Create multiple sections** for the content, such as "Upcoming Events," "Featured Articles," and "News from the Community."
4. **Insert images and graphics** relevant to each section to enhance the visual appeal.
5. **Use columns** for the main content of your newsletter.
6. **Format the text:**
   - Use headings and subheadings to organize the content.
   - Apply bullet points for lists and numbered lists where necessary.
   - Change the font and size for each section to add variety.
7. **Save and review your newsletter.**

Goal: This exercise will help you build a well-organized newsletter with multiple sections, enhanced by images and appropriate formatting.

Conclusion

By completing these practice exercises and sample projects, you'll gain a deeper understanding of Microsoft Word's functionality and how to apply it in practical situations. With these skills, you'll be well-equipped to create professional-looking documents, whether you're preparing a resume, drafting a letter, or working on a complex report. Keep practicing, experimenting with different features, and soon you'll be creating Word documents like a pro!

Chapter 21: Glossary of Terms

In this section, we will define some of the most commonly used terms in Microsoft Word. Understanding these terms will empower you to navigate the software with ease and make the most of its many features. Whether you're creating documents, formatting text, or collaborating with others, knowing the terminology will enhance your overall experience.

1. Alignment

Alignment refers to how text is positioned on the page in relation to the margins. Microsoft Word provides several alignment options:

- **Left Alignment**: Text is aligned to the left margin, creating a straight line on the left side of the page.
- **Center Alignment**: Text is centered between the left and right margins, creating equal spacing on both sides.
- **Right Alignment**: Text is aligned to the right margin, creating a straight line on the right side of the page.
- **Justified Alignment**: Text is stretched to fill the entire width of the page, with the spaces between words adjusted accordingly.

2. AutoCorrect

AutoCorrect is a feature that automatically corrects common spelling and grammatical errors as you type. For example, if you type "teh" instead of "the," Word will automatically correct it. AutoCorrect can also be customized to fix specific words or phrases that you often mistype.

3. Backstage View

Backstage View is a feature accessible from the **File** tab that gives you access to document management options, such as **Save**, **Open**, **Print**, and **Share**. It's essentially the place where you manage your files and settings for the current document.

4. Blank Document

A blank document is a new, empty page that you can use to create content from scratch. You can either open a blank document by default when Word starts, or you can choose to open a blank document from the **File** tab.

5. Clipboard

The Clipboard is a temporary storage area in your computer's memory where data is kept when you use the **Cut**, **Copy**, and **Paste** commands. Items you copy or cut are stored in the clipboard until you paste them somewhere else. You can copy and paste text, images, or files.

6. Comment

A comment is a text annotation that can be added to a document without modifying the content. Comments are often used for reviewing or providing feedback. In Microsoft Word, comments are typically placed in the margin and can be reviewed, edited, or deleted by anyone who has access to the document.

7. Copy

The **Copy** function is used to duplicate text, images, or other objects without removing them from the original location. Once you copy an item, it is temporarily stored in the Clipboard and can be pasted into a different location.

8. Cut

The **Cut** function is used to remove text, images, or other objects from their current location and store them temporarily in the Clipboard. You can then paste the cut item elsewhere in the document.

9. Document View

Document View refers to the way your document appears on the screen. Word offers several view options to help you work more efficiently:

- **Print Layout**: Shows the document as it will appear when printed, including headers, footers, and page breaks.
- **Web Layout**: Displays how the document will look in a web browser.
- **Outline**: Provides an outline view of the document, which helps with structuring and organizing content.
- **Draft**: A simplified view without page breaks or other elements, useful for focused writing.

10. Document Theme

A **Document Theme** is a set of predefined formatting styles, such as fonts, colors, and effects, that gives your document a cohesive look. By applying a theme, you can quickly change the visual style of your document to create a professional appearance.

11. Font

The **Font** is the style or design of the text in your document. Microsoft Word offers numerous fonts, each with different characteristics (e.g., **Arial**, **Times New Roman**, **Calibri**). The font can be customized in terms of size, style, weight (bold, italic), and color.

12. Footer

A **Footer** is text or other content that appears at the bottom of every page in a document. It often contains elements like page numbers, document titles, or copyright information. You can insert a footer via the **Insert** tab.

13. Format Painter

The **Format Painter** is a tool in Microsoft Word that allows you to copy the formatting of text or objects and apply it to other areas of your document. To use it, select the formatted text or object, click the Format Painter button, and then drag to the target area.

14. Header

A **Header** is similar to a footer, but it appears at the top of each page in a document. Like the footer, it can contain page numbers, titles, author names, or any other relevant information. Headers are useful for professional-looking documents and reports.

15. Hyperlink

A **Hyperlink** is a clickable link that directs the user to a different location within the same document or to an external web page. Hyperlinks are often used for referencing, citations, or navigation within longer documents.

16. Indentation

Indentation is the space added to the beginning of a paragraph or text block. There are several types of indentation:

- **First Line Indent**: The first line of a paragraph is indented.
- **Hanging Indent**: All lines except the first line are indented.
- **Left Indent**: The entire paragraph is indented from the left margin.
- **Right Indent**: The entire paragraph is indented from the right margin.

17. Justification

Justification is the process of adjusting the spaces between words and letters so that the text aligns evenly along both the left and right margins. Justified text creates a clean, uniform appearance, but it may result in inconsistent spacing between words if not done carefully.

18. Mail Merge

Mail Merge is a tool that allows you to create personalized documents for multiple recipients at once. This feature is commonly used for creating bulk letters, labels, or envelopes. You can import recipient data from external sources such as **Excel** or **Access** to generate a customized document for each person.

19. Margin

Margins are the blank spaces around the edges of a page. Microsoft Word allows you to adjust the margins to control the amount of space on each side of the page. You can modify margins in the **Layout** tab, and standard margin sizes include 1 inch for all sides.

20. Paragraph Styles

Paragraph Styles are predefined formatting options that apply to entire paragraphs. These styles control elements like font size, color, alignment, and line spacing. By applying a paragraph style, you can quickly change the appearance of a paragraph without manually adjusting each setting.

21. Paste

The **Paste** function is used to insert text, images, or objects that have been copied or cut from another location. To paste an item, simply place the cursor where you want it and select **Paste** from the **Home** tab or use the **Ctrl+V** keyboard shortcut.

22. Ribbon

The **Ribbon** is the main interface in Microsoft Word, located at the top of the screen. It contains tabs such as **Home, Insert**, and **Design,** each with its own set of tools and commands. The Ribbon is designed to make it easy to access the various functions and features Word offers.

23. Spell Check

Spell Check is a feature in Word that automatically scans your document for spelling mistakes and underlines them with a red squiggly line. You can then right-click the underlined word to choose a suggested correction or ignore the error.

24. Template

A **Template** is a pre-designed document that contains predefined formatting, styles, and sometimes even sample content. Templates are useful for creating documents that need to follow a specific format, such as resumes, newsletters, or business reports.

25. Text Box

A **Text Box** is a container used to hold text in a specific area of a document. Text boxes allow you to position text anywhere on the page and are commonly used for creating newsletters, flyers, and other types of documents with complex layouts.

26. Track Changes

Track Changes is a feature that allows you to monitor edits and modifications made to a document. This feature is commonly used in collaborative environments to track revisions, suggestions, and comments. Changes are marked up with colored highlights, strikethroughs, and underlines, making it easy to see what has been added or removed.

27. Word Count

Word Count is a tool that provides a detailed count of words, characters, paragraphs, and pages in your document. You can view the word count from the **Review** tab or check the information in the status bar at the bottom of the screen.

Chapter 22: Frequently Asked Questions (FAQs)

As you embark on your journey with Microsoft Word, it's natural to have questions about how to use certain features or troubleshoot common issues. This chapter addresses some of the most frequently asked questions by beginners, helping you navigate through any challenges you might encounter while using the program. Let's explore these queries and provide clear, easy-to-understand answers.

1. How do I get started with Microsoft Word for the first time?

When you first open Microsoft Word, you'll be greeted by the **Home screen**, which offers several options. You can start a new document by clicking on **Blank Document**, or you can use one of the pre-built **templates** available. If you're new to the software, it's a good idea to start with a blank document to familiarize yourself with the interface and basic features.

Once your document is open, take a moment to explore the **Ribbon**, which houses all the essential tools you'll need. Start by typing some text and experimenting with basic formatting like font changes, text alignment, and paragraph spacing. As you grow more comfortable, you can explore additional features like inserting images, tables, and even creating headings and footers.

2. What's the difference between saving and saving as?

The **Save** option is used to save any changes to the document you're currently working on. Once you've saved your document for the first time, clicking **Save** again will automatically overwrite the file with your most recent changes.

On the other hand, **Save As** is used when you want to create a new version of the document or save it in a different format. For example, you might want to save your Word document as a **PDF** or store it in a different location. To do this, click **File > Save As**, choose the location where you'd like to save the file, and select the desired format.

3. How do I undo or redo changes in my document?

Mistakes are a part of the process, and thankfully, Microsoft Word makes it easy to fix them. To **undo** an action, simply press **Ctrl+Z** (or **Cmd+Z** on a Mac). This will reverse your most recent change, whether you've deleted text, applied formatting, or made any other edits.

If you change your mind and want to **redo** the action, press **Ctrl+Y** (or **Cmd+Y** on a Mac). This will restore the change you previously undid.

You can also use the **Undo** and **Redo** buttons in the toolbar at the top of the screen (usually represented by a backward arrow for undo and a forward arrow for redo).

4. How do I insert a table into my document?

Inserting a table in Microsoft Word is a simple task. Follow these steps to add a table to your document:

1. Navigate to the **Insert** tab in the Ribbon.
2. Click the **Table** button, and a grid will appear.
3. Hover over the grid and select the number of rows and columns you need by clicking on the boxes.
4. Once the table is inserted, you can easily adjust the size of the rows and columns by dragging the borders.

You can also right-click within the table to add or remove rows and columns, or you can format the table using the **Table Design** options.

5. How do I change the page orientation from portrait to landscape?

To change the orientation of your document:

1. Go to the **Layout** tab on the Ribbon.
2. In the **Page Setup** group, click on the **Orientation** button.
3. Choose either **Portrait** (vertical) or **Landscape** (horizontal) orientation, depending on how you want your page to be displayed.

Changing the page orientation is especially useful for documents that require wide tables or charts, such as reports or presentations.

6. How do I insert a picture into my document?

To add a picture to your document, follow these steps:

1. Click on the **Insert** tab.
2. Click the **Pictures** button.
3. You'll be given the option to choose a picture from your computer or from online sources. Select the desired image, and it will be inserted into your document.

Once the image is in your document, you can resize it by clicking on the image and dragging its corners. You can also use the **Picture Tools** to adjust the brightness, contrast, and crop the image if necessary.

7. Can I create a table of contents in Word?

Yes, you can easily create a table of contents (TOC) in Microsoft Word, especially for longer documents like reports, theses, or books. To add a TOC:

1. Place your cursor where you want the table of contents to appear.
2. Go to the **References** tab and click on **Table of Contents**.
3. Choose from one of the built-in styles or select **Custom Table of Contents** to customize it further.

Word uses the headings in your document to generate the table of contents, so make sure to use the **Heading 1**, **Heading 2**, and **Heading 3** styles for the sections and subsections you want included in the TOC.

8. How do I password-protect my document?

To add a password to your document to prevent unauthorized access:

1. Click on the **File** tab.
2. Select **Info,** and then click on **Protect Document.**
3. Choose **Encrypt with Password.**
4. Enter your desired password and click **OK**. You will be prompted to confirm the password.

Be sure to choose a strong password and remember it, as losing it can prevent you from accessing the document in the future.

9. How do I recover an unsaved document?

Microsoft Word has a built-in feature that automatically saves your work as you go, especially if you're using OneDrive or a similar cloud-based service. If your computer crashes or you forget to save your document, Word may still have a recovery option available.

1. Open Microsoft Word and go to the **File** tab.
2. Click on **Open** and then **Recent**.
3. Scroll to the bottom and click on **Recover Unsaved Documents**.

If Word has an autosaved version of your document, it will appear here, and you can restore it to continue working.

10. What is the difference between a .docx and a .doc file?

The main difference between these two file extensions lies in the version of Word that created them:

- **.docx**: This is the default file format for Word documents starting from Word 2007 and onward. It's based on the Office Open XML format, which allows for smaller file sizes and better compatibility with other software.
- **.doc**: This is the older format used by Word 2003 and earlier versions. It's less efficient and not as widely used today.

When working with documents in Word 2007 or later, it's best to use the **.docx** format. However, if you need to share documents with users of older versions of Word, you may need to save your document in the **.doc** format.

11. How can I add comments or suggestions in my document?

If you're collaborating on a document or need to leave feedback, Word makes it easy to add comments:

1. Highlight the text or area you want to comment on.
2. Go to the **Review** tab on the Ribbon.
3. Click **New Comment**.

4. Type your comment in the sidebar that appears.

This feature is particularly useful for sharing thoughts or providing feedback in a shared document. You can also reply to comments made by others, making it easier to collaborate.

12. How do I print my document?

Before printing your document, you can preview it to make sure everything looks correct:

1. Click on the **File** tab and select **Print**.
2. In the **Print Preview** window, review your document to ensure it's formatted correctly.
3. You can select your printer, adjust settings like page range and number of copies, and customize other print options.
4. Once you're ready, click **Print**.

Index

www.ingramcontent.com/pod-product-compliance
Lightning Source LLC
LaVergne TN
LVHW051323050326
832903LV00031B/3335